RUDOLF STEINER

AT THE GATES OF
SPIRITUAL SCIENCE

Fourteen lectures given in
Stuttgart

22 August to 4 September, 1906

Revised translation by E.H.G. and C.D.

Rudolf Steiner Press

First Edition in English 1970
Second Impression (paperback) 1976

Translated from a text consisting of notes which had been made by
a member of the audience and not revised by the lecturer. The
volume in the Complete Edition in German of Rudolf Steiner's
works containing this text (see Prefatory Note) is entitled: *Vor dem
Tore der Theosophie* (No. 95).

This English edition is published in agreement with the *Rudolf
Steiner-Nachlassverwaltung*, Dornach, Switzerland.

ISBN 0 85440 306 X

MADE AND PRINTED IN GREAT BRITAIN BY
BRIER PRESS LTD.
WEST END ROAD, HIGH WYCOMBE, BUCKS.

CONTENTS

PREFATORY NOTE

In *The Story of my Life* Rudolf Steiner describes how at the turn of the century he was invited to give lectures to members of the Theosophical Society. "I explained that I could speak only of what lived in me as Spiritual Science." Within the German Section of that Society—founded soon after the lectures began—"I was able to expound my anthroposophical activity to constantly increasing audiences. No-one was left in any doubt that I was going to bring before the Theosophical Society only the results of my own clairvoyant research."

The lectures given in the winter of 1900-1901 were assembled by Rudolf Steiner in the book *Mysticism and Modern Thought.* He had given in them only the fruits of his own spiritual vision, and these were accepted in the Theosophical Society. "In addressing the theosophical public, which was then the only available public and was continually searching for knowledge of the spirit, there was no longer any reason for me not to present this knowledge in my own way. I subscribed to no sectarian dogma; I remained an individual who believed he was able to speak of what he had himself experienced as the spiritual world."

This independence—combined with symptoms of decline in the Theosophical Society at that time—led to the expulsion of the German Section in 1913. "We were obliged to found the Anthroposophical Society as an independent body."

Hence the terms "Theosophy" and "theosophical" in these lectures should be understood as applying to the results of Rudolf Steiner's own spiritual-scientific research—results for which he otherwise used the terms "Anthroposophy" and "anthroposophical".

THE BEING OF MAN

These lectures are intended to give a general survey of the whole field of theosophical thought. Theosophy has not always been taught as it is today, in lectures and books that are accessible to everyone. It used to be taught only in small, intimate groups, and knowledge of it was confined to circles of Initiates, to occult brotherhoods; ordinary people were meant to have only the fruits of this knowledge. Not much was known about the knowledge or the activities of these Initiates, or about the places where they worked. Those whom the world recognises as the great men of history were not really the greatest; the greatest, the Initiates, kept in the background.

In the course of the eighteenth century, on a quite unnoticed occasion, an Initiate made brief acquaintance with a writer, and spoke words to which the writer paid no special attention at the time. But they worked on in him and later gave rise to potent ideas, the fruits of which are in countless hands today. The writer was Jean-Jacques Rousseau. He was not an Initiate, but his knowledge derived from one.

Here is another example. Jacob Boehme, a shoemaker's apprentice, was sitting alone one day in the shop, where he was not allowed to sell anything himself. A person came in, made a deep impression upon him, spoke a few words, and went away. Immediately afterwards, Boehme heard his name being called: "Jacob, Jacob, today you are small, but one day you will be great. Take heed of what you have seen today!" A secret attraction remained between Boehme and his visitor, who was a great Initiate, and the source of Boehme's powerful inspirations.

There were still other means by which an Initiate could work in those times. For instance, a man might receive a letter intended to bring about action of some kind. The recipient might perhaps be a Minister, someone who had the power but not the ideas to carry out a particular project. The letter might be about something, perhaps a request, which had nothing to do with its real purpose. But there might have been a certain way of reading the letter. For example, if four words out of five were deleted and the last word left, these fifth words would make a new sequence conveying what was to be done, although the recipient, of course, was not aware of it. If the words were the right ones, they achieved their object, even though the reader had not consciously taken in their meaning. Trithemius of Sponheim, a German scholar who was also an Initiate and the teacher of Agrippa von Nettesheim, used this method. Given the right key, you will find in his works much that is taught today in Theosophy.

In earlier times, only a few who had undergone adequate preparation could be initiated. Why was this secrecy necessary? In order to ensure the right attitude towards knowledge, it had to be restricted to those who were adequately prepared; the others received its blessings only. This knowledge was not intended to satisfy idle curiosity or inquisitiveness; it was meant to be put to work, to have a practical influence on political and social institutions in the world. In this way all the great advances in the development of humanity owe their origin to impulses issuing from occultism. For this reason, too, all those who were to be instructed in theosophical teachings were obliged to undergo severe tests and trials to prove their worthiness; and then they were initiated step by step, and led upwards quite slowly.

This method has been abandoned in modern times; the more elementary teachings are now given out publicly. This is necessary because the earlier methods, whereby only the fruits of the teaching were allowed to reach humanity, would fail. Among these earlier methods we must include religions, and this wisdom was a constituent part of all of them. Nowadays, however, we hear of a conflict between

8

knowledge and faith. What is necessary today is to attain to higher knowledge by the paths of learning.

The decisive event which led to the making public of this knowledge, however, was the invention of printing. Previously, theosophical teaching had been passed on orally from one person to another, and nobody who was unripe or unworthy would hear of it. But knowledge of the material world was spread abroad and made popular through books; hence arose the conflict between knowledge and faith. Issues such as this have made it necessary for much of the great treasure of occult knowledge of all ages to be made accessible to the public. Whence does man originate? What is his goal? What lies hidden behind his visible form? What happens after death?—all these questions have to be answered, and answered not by theories and hypotheses and surmises, but by the relevant facts.

The purpose of occult science has always been to unravel the riddle of man. Everything said in these lectures will be from the standpoint of practical occultism; they will contain nothing that is mere theory and cannot be put into practice. Such theories have found their way into theosophical literature because in the beginning the people who wrote the books did not understand clearly what they were writing about. This kind of writing may indeed be very useful for curiosity-addicts; but Theosophy must be carried into real life.

Let us first consider the nature and being of man. When someone comes into our presence, we first of all see through our sense-organs what Theosophy calls the physical body. Man has this body in common with the whole world around him; and although the physical body is only a small part of what man really is, it is the only part of which ordinary science takes account. But we must go deeper. Even superficial observation will make it clear that this physical body has very special qualities. There are plenty of other things which you can see and touch; every stone is after all a physical body. But man can move, feel and think; he grows, takes nourishment, propagates his kind. None of this is true of a stone, but some of it is certainly true of plants and animals. Man has in common with the plants his capacity to nourish himself, to grow and propagate; if he were like a stone, with only a physical body, none of this would be possible. He must therefore possess something which enables him to use substances and their forces in such a way that they become for him the means of growth and so forth. This is the etheric body.

Man has a physical body in common with the mineral kingdom, and an etheric body in common with the plant and animal kingdoms. Ordinary observation can confirm that. But there is another way whereby we can convince ourselves of the existence of an etheric body, although only those who have developed their higher senses have this faculty. These higher senses are no more than a higher development of what is dormant in every human being. It is rather like a man born blind being operated on so that he can see. The difference is that not everyone born blind can be successfully operated on, whereas everyone can develop the spiritual senses if he has the necessary patience and goes through the proper preliminary training. A very definite form of higher perception is needed to understand this principle of life, growth, nutrition and propagation. The example of hypnotism can help us to show what this means.

Hypnotism, which has always been known to the Initiates, implies a condition of consciousness different from that of ordinary sleep. There must be a close *rapport* between the hypnotiser and his subject. Two types of suggestion are involved—positive and negative. The first makes a person see what is not there, while the second diverts his attention from something that is present and is thus only an intensification of a condition familiar enough in everyday life when our attention is diverted from an object so that we do not see it, although our eyes are open. This happens to us involuntarily every day when we are wholly absorbed in something. Theosophy will have nothing to do with conditions where consciousness is dimmed and dulled. To grasp theosophical truths a man must be quite as much in control of his senses when investigating higher worlds as he is when investigating ordinary matters. The serious dangers inherent in Initiation can affect him only if his consciousness is dimmed.

Anyone who wants to know the nature of the etheric body by direct vision must be able to maintain his ordinary consciousness intact and "suggest away" the physical body by the strength of his own will. The gap left will, however, not be empty; he will see before him the etheric body glowing with a reddish-blue light like a phantom, but with radiance a little darker than young peach blossom. We never see an etheric body if we "suggest away" a crystal; but in the case of a plant or animal we do, for it is the etheric body that is responsible for nutrition, growth and reproduction.

Man, of course, has other faculties as well. He can feel pleasure and pain, which the plant cannot do. The Initiate can discover this by his own experience, for he can identify himself with the plant. Animals can feel pleasure and pain, and thus have a further principle in common with man: the astral body. The astral body is the seat of everything we know as desire, passion, and so forth. This is clear to straightforward observation as an inner experience, but for the Initiate the astral body can become an outer reality. The Initiate sees this third member of man as an egg-shaped cloud which not only surrounds the body, but permeates it. If we "suggest away" the physical body and also the etheric body, what we shall see will be a delicate cloud of light, inwardly full of movement. Within this cloud or aura the Initiate sees every desire, every impulse, as colour and form in the astral body. For example, he sees intense passion flashing like rays of lightning out of the astral body.

In animals the basic colour of the astral body varies with the species: a lion's astral body has a different basic colour from that of a lamb. Even in human beings the colour is not always the same, and if you train yourself to be sensitive to

11

delicate nuances, you will be able to recognise a man's temperament and general disposition by his aura. Nervous people have a dappled aura; the spots are not static but keep on lighting up and fading away. This is always so, and is why the aura cannot be painted.

But man is distinguished from the animal in still another way. This brings us to the fourth member of man's being, which comes to expression in a name different from all other names. I can say "I" only of myself. In the whole of language there is no other name which cannot be applied by all and sundry to the same object. It is not so with "I"; a man can say it only of himself. Initiates have always been aware of this. Hebrew Initiates spoke of the "inexpressible name of God", of the God who dwells in man, for the name can be uttered only by the soul for this same soul. It must sound forth from the soul and the soul must give itself its own name; no other soul can utter it. Hence the emotion of wonder which thrilled through the listeners when the name "Jahve" was uttered, for Jahve or Jehovah signifies "I" or "I AM". In the name which the soul uses of itself, the God begins to speak within that individual soul.

This attribute makes man superior to the animals. We must realise the tremendous significance of this word. When Jean Paul had discovered the "I" within himself, he knew that he had experienced his immortal being.

This again presents itself to the seer in a peculiar form. When he studies the astral body, everything appears in perpetual movement except for one small space, shaped like a somewhat elongated blue oval, situated at the base of the nose, behind the brow. This is to be seen in human beings only—more clearly in the less civilised peoples, most clearly of all in savages at the lowest level of culture. Actually there is nothing there but an empty space. Just as the empty centre of a flame appears blue when seen through the light around it, so this empty space appears blue because of the auric light streaming around it. This is the outer form of expression of the "I".

12

Every human being has these four members; but there is a difference between a primitive savage and a civilised European, and also between the latter and a Francis of Assisi, or a Schiller. A refinement of the moral nature produces finer colours in the aura; an increase in the power of discrimination between good and evil also shows itself in a refinement of the aura. In the process of becoming civilised the "I" has worked upon the astral body and ennobled the desires. The higher the moral and intellectual development of a man, the more will his "I" have worked upon the astral body. The seer can distinguish between a developed and an undeveloped human being.

Whatever part of the astral body has been thus transformed by the "I" is called *Manas*. Manas is the fifth member of man's nature. A man has just so much of Manas as he has created by his own efforts; part of his astral body is therefore always Manas. But a man is not able to exercise an immediate influence upon the etheric body, although in the same way that he can raise himself to a higher moral level, he can also learn to work upon the etheric body. Then he will be called a Chela, a pupil. He can thus attain mastery over the etheric body, and what he has transformed in this body by his own efforts is called *Buddhi*. This is the sixth member of man's nature, the transformed etheric body.

Such a Chela can be recognised by a certain sign. An ordinary man shows no resemblance either in temperament or form to his previous incarnation. The Chela has the same habits, the same temperament as in the previous incarnation. This similarity remains because he has worked consciously on the etheric body, the bearer of the forces of growth and reproduction.

The highest achievement open to man on this Earth is to work right down into his physical body. That is the most difficult task of all. In order to have an effect upon the physical body itself, a man must learn to control the breath and the circulation, to follow consciously the activity of the nerves, and to regulate the processes of thought. In theosophical language, a man who has reached this stage is called an Adept; he will then have developed in himself what we call *Atma*. Atma is the seventh member of man's being.

In every human being four members are fully formed, the fifth only partly, the sixth and seventh in rudiment only. Physical body, etheric body, astral body, "I" or Ego, Manas, Buddhi, Atma—these are the seven members of man's nature; through them he can participate in three worlds.

THE THREE WORLDS

When one speaks of the knowledge of higher realms possessed by Initiates but not yet accessible to ordinary people, one often hears an objection to the following effect: What use to us is this knowledge you say you have of higher worlds if we cannot look into these worlds for ourselves?

I will reply by quoting some beautiful words by a young contemporary whose destiny it has been to become widely known—Helen Keller. In her second year she became blind and deaf, and even in her seventh year this human child was little more than an animal. Then she met a teacher of genius, a woman who gave her love, and now, at the age of twenty-six, Helen Keller is certainly one of the most cultured of her compatriots. She has studied the sciences and is astonishingly well read; she is acquainted with the poets, both classical and modern; she also has a good knowledge of the philosophers, Plato, Spinoza and so on. Although the realms of light and sound are for ever closed to her, she retains an impressive courage for living and takes delight in the beauty and splendour of the world. In her book, *Optimism*, there are some memorable sentences. "Night and darkness lay around me for years and then came one who taught me, and instead of night and darkness I found peace and hope." Or again, "I have won my way to heaven by thinking and feeling." Only one thing could be given to her, deprived as she was of sight and hearing, with the sense-world accessible to her only through the communications of others. The lofty thoughts of men of genius have flowed into her soul, and through the reports of those who can speak with knowledge she shares in our familiar world.

That is the situation of anyone who hears of higher

worlds only through the communications of others. From this comparison we can see how important such communications are for a person who is himself not yet able to see into these higher worlds. But there is a difference here. Helen Keller has to say to herself: "I shall never be able to see the world with my own eyes." But every normal person can say to himself: "I shall be able to see into the higher worlds when the eyes of my spirit are opened." The spiritual eyes and ears of everyone can be opened, if he brings enough patience and perseverance to the task.

Others again ask: How long will it take me to achieve this faculty of spiritual sight? To this an admirable reply has been given by that notable thinker, Subba Row. He says: One man will achieve it in seventy incarnations, another in seven; one in seven years, another in seven months or seven days or seven hours; or it will come, as the Bible says, "like a thief in the night". As I have said, the eyes of the spirit can be opened in every person, if he has the necessary energy and patience. Everyone, accordingly, can derive joy and hope from the communications of another, for what we are told about the higher worlds is not mere theory, unrelated to life. As its fruits it brings us two things we must have if we are to lay hold of life in the right way—strength and security—and both are given in the highest measure. Strength comes from the impulses of the higher worlds; security comes when we are consciously aware that we have been created from out of the invisible worlds. Moreover, nobody has true knowledge of the visible world unless he knows something also of two other worlds.

The three worlds are:

1. The physical world, the scene of human life.
2. The astral world or the world of soul.
3. The devachanic world or world of spirit.

These three worlds are not spatially separate. We are surrounded by the things of the physical world which we perceive with our ordinary senses: but the astral world is in

16

this same space; we live in the other two worlds, the astral and devachanic worlds, at the same time as we live in the physical world. The three worlds are wherever we ourselves are, only we do not yet see the two higher worlds—just as a blind man does not see the physical world. But when the "senses of the soul" are opened, the new world, with its new characteristics and new beings, emerges. In proportion as a man acquires new senses, so are new phenomena revealed to him.

Let us turn now to closer study of the three worlds. The physical world need not be specially characterised. Everyone is familiar with it and with the physical laws which obtain there.

We get to know the astral world only after death, unless as initiates we are already aware of it. Anyone whose senses are opened to the astral world will at first be bewildered, because there is really nothing in the physical world with which he can compare it. The astral world has a whole range of characteristics of its own and he has to learn many new things. One of the most perplexing aspects of this world is that all things appear reversed, in a sort of mirror-reflection, and he has to get used to seeing everything in a new way. For instance, he has to learn to read numbers backwards. We are accustomed to read the figures 3, 4, 5, as 345 but in the astral world we have to read them backwards as 543. Everything appears as its mirror-reflection, and it is essential to be aware of this.

The same law applies also to higher things—in the field of morality, for instance. People do not at first understand this. It may happen that they see themselves surrounded by black, malignant forms which threaten and terrify them—this happens with very many people and they mostly have no idea what it signifies. The fact is that these figures are their own impulses, desires and passions, which live in what we call the astral body. Ordinary people do not see their own passions, but these may sometimes become visible as a result of processes active in the brain and soul, and then they appear as

17

mirror-images. You see the mirror-images of your desires in the same way as when looking into a mirror you see reflected images of the objects around you. Everything that comes out of you seems to be going into you. Further, time and events move backwards. In the physical world you see first the hen and then the egg. In the astral world you see the egg and then the hen that laid it. Time in the astral moves backwards: you see first the effect and then the cause. This explains how prophecy is possible—if it were not for this reversal of the time-sequence it would be impossible to foresee events.

It is by no means useless to recognise these peculiarities of the astral world. Many myths and legends are concerned with them in a wonderfully wise way—for example, the story of the choice of Hercules. Hercules, we are told, once felt himself to be in the presence of two female forms, one beautiful and seductive who promised him pleasure, good fortune and happiness, the other plain and serious, who promised him hard work, weariness and renunciation. The two forms represent vice and virtue, and the story tells us quite rightly how the two natures appeared to Hercules in the astral, one urging him to evil, the other to good. In the mirror-picture they appear as the forms of two women with opposite qualities—vice as beautiful, voluptuous and fascinating, virtue as ugly and repulsive. All such images appear in the astral world reversed. Scholars attribute these legends to the folk-spirit (*Volksgeist*) but that is not true. Nor do these legends grow up by chance: the great Initiates created them out of their wisdom and imparted them to humanity. All myths, legends, religions and folk-poetry help towards the solution of the riddles of the world, and are founded on the inspiration of Initiates.

The higher worlds convey to us the impulses and powers for living, and in this way we get a basis for morality. Schopenhauer once said: "To preach morality is easy, to find a foundation for it, difficult." But without a true foundation we can never make morality our own. People

18

often say: Why worry about the knowledge of higher worlds so long as we are good men and have moral principles? In the long run no mere preaching of morality will be effective; but a knowledge of the truth gives morality a sound basis. To preach morality is like preaching to a stove about its duty to provide warmth and heat, while not giving it any coal. If we want a firm foundation for morality, we must supply the soul with fuel in the form of knowledge of the truth.

In occultism there is a saying which can now be made known: In the astral world, every lie is a murder. The full significance of this saying can be appreciated only by someone who has knowledge of the higher worlds. How readily people say: "Oh, that is only a thought or a feeling; it exists only in the soul. To box someone's ears is wrong, but a bad thought does no harm." No proverb is more untrue than the one which says: "You don't have to pay for your thoughts." Every thought and every feeling is a reality, and if I let myself think that someone is a bad man or that I don't like him, then for anyone who can see into the astral world the thought is like an arrow or thunderbolt hurled against the other's astral body and injuring it as a gunshot would. I repeat: every thought and every feeling is a reality, and for anyone with astral vision it is often much worse to see someone harbouring bad thoughts about another than to see him inflicting physical harm. When we make this truth known we are not preaching morality but laying a solid foundation for it. If we speak the truth about our neighbour, we are creating a thought which the seer can recognise by its colour and form, and it will be a thought which gives strength to our neighbour. Any thought containing truth finds its way to the being whom it concerns and lends him strength and vigour. If I speak lies about him, I pour out a hostile force which destroys and may even kill him. In this way every lie is an act of murder. Every spoken truth creates a life-promoting element; every lie, an element hostile to life. Anyone who knows this will take much greater care to speak the truth and avoid lies than if he is merely preached at and told he must be nice and truthful.

The astral world is composed in the main of forms and colours similar to those of the physical world, but the colours float freely, like flames, and are not always associated with a particular object, as they are in the physical world. There is one phenomenon in the physical world—the rainbow—which can give you some idea of these floating colours. But the astral colour-images move freely in space; they flicker like a sea of colours, with varying and ever-changing forms and lines.

The pupil gradually comes to recognise a certain resemblance between the physical and astral worlds. At first the sea of colour appears uncontrolled, unattached to any objects; but then the flakes of colour merge together and attach themselves, not indeed to objects but to beings. Whereas previously only a floating shape was apparent, spiritual beings, called gods or Devas, now reveal themselves through the colours. The astral world, then, is a world of beings who speak to us through colour.

The astral world is the world of colours; above it is the devachanic world, the world of spirits. The pupil learns to recognise the spiritual world through a quite definite event: he comes to understand the profound utterance of Indian wisdom, "Tat tvam asi"—"That thou art". Much has been written about this saying, but to the pupil its true meaning becomes clear for the first time when he passes from the astral world into the world of Devachan. Then for a moment he sees his physical form outside himself and says, "That thou art"; and then he is in the world of Devachan. And so another world appears to him; after the world of colours comes the world of musical sounds which in a certain sense was there already without the significance it now has. The world of Devachan is a world of sounds—the sounds which Pythagoras called the music of the spheres. The heavenly bodies as they pursue their courses, can be heard resounding. Here we recognise the harmony of the Cosmos and we find that everything lives in music. Goethe, as an Initiate, speaks of the Sun resounding; he indicates the secret of Devachan. When Faust is in heaven, in the spiritual world, surrounded by Devas, the Sun and the spheres speak in music:

> The day-star, sonorous as of old
>> Goes his predestined way along,
> And round his path is thunder rolled,
>> While sister-spheres join rival song.

> *Faust,* Part I, Act I, Prologue in Heaven.
> Translation by Philip Wayne.
> Penguin Classics, 1949.

Goethe means the spirit of the Sun, which really does sound forth to us in music if we are in the world of Devachan. We can see that this is indeed what Goethe means because he keeps the same image later, in the Second Part of *Faust,* when Faust is again caught up into this world:

> Hark! the Hóurs, with furious winging,
> Bear to spirit-ears the ringing
> Rumour of the new day-springing.
> Gates of rock grind back asunder,
> Phoebus comes with wheels of thunder:
> Light spreads tumult through the air.
> Loud are trump and timbrel sounded,
> Eyes are dazed and ears astounded,
> Sounds unheard of none may hear.

> *Faust,* Part II, Act I.
> Translation by Philip Wayne.
> Penguin Classics, 1959.

When we enter the devachanic world the astral world remains fully present; we hear the devachanic, and we see the astral, but under a changed aspect, offering us a remarkable spectacle. We see everything in the negative, as though on a photographic plate. Where a physical object exists, there is

21

nothing; what is light in the physical world appears dark, and vice versa. We see things, too, in their complementary colours: yellow instead of blue, green instead of red.

In the first region of Devachan we see the archetypes of the physical world in so far as it has no life—the archetypes, that is, of the minerals—but also the archetypes of plants, animals and men in so far as their physical forms are concerned. This is the region which provides as it were the basic skeleton of Spirit-land. It can be compared with the solid land on Earth and is therefore called the "Continental Mass" of Devachan. When a man is observed over there by an Initiate, the physical space he occupies appears dark, but round him is a radiant halo.

When our senses have become more delicately organised, the archetypes of life are added: everything that has life flows over the Earth like water. Here the minerals cannot be seen because they have no vibrant life; but plants, animals and men can be seen very well. Life circulates in Devachan like blood in the body. This second region is called the "Ocean" of Devachan.

In a third region, the "Atmosphere", we encounter feelings and emotions, pleasure and pain, wherever they are active in the physical. Physical forms then are like solid foundations, the Continents, of Devachan. Everything that has life forms its Ocean. Everything that pleasure and pain signify are its Atmosphere. The content of all that is suffered or enjoyed on Earth, by men or by animals, is displayed here. Thus to the Initiate a battle appears like a great thunderstorm, fiery flashes of lightning, powerful claps of thunder. He sees, not the physical actions that occur in the battle, but the passions of the opposing armies, and these appear to him like the heavy clouds and lightning-flashes of a thunderstorm.

The fourth region transcends everything that might still have existed even if there had been no mankind. It includes all man's original thoughts which enable him to bring something new into the world and to act upon it, no matter whether the thoughts are those of an ignorant or a learned man, of a poet or a peasant. They need not involve any great discoveries; they may belong to everyday life.

After these four regions we come to the boundary of the spiritual world. Just as the sky at night looks like a hollow globe encircled by stars, so it is with this boundary of Devachan. But it is a highly significant boundary; it forms what we call the Akasha Chronicle. Whatever a person has done and accomplished is recorded in that imperishable book of history even if there is no mention of it in our history books. We can experience there everything that has ever been done on Earth by conscious beings. Suppose the seer wants to know something about Caesar: he will take some little incident from history as a starting-point on which to concentrate. This he does "in the spirit"; and then around him appear pictures of all that Caesar did and of all that happened round him—how he led his legions, fought his battles, won his victories.

All this happens in a remarkable way: the seer does not see an abstract script; everything passes before him in silhouettes and pictures, and what he sees is not what actually happened in space; it is something quite different. When Caesar gained one of his victories, he was of course thinking; and all that happened around entered into his thoughts; every movement of an army exists in thought. The Akasha Chronicle therefore shows his intentions, all that he thought and imagined as he was leading his legions; and their thoughts, too, are shown. It is a true picture of what happened, and whatever conscious beings have experienced is depicted there. (Plants, of course, cannot be seen.) Hence the Initiate can read off the whole past history of humanity —but he must first learn how to do it.

These Akasha pictures speak a confusing language, because the Akasha is alive. The Akasha image of Caesar must not be compared with Caesar's individuality, which may already have been reincarnated again. This sort of confusion may very easily arise if we have gained access to the Akasha pictures by external means. Hence they often play a part in spiritualistic séances. The spiritualist imagines he is seeing a man who has died, when it is really only his Akasha picture. Thus a picture of Goethe may appear as he was in 1796, and if we are not properly informed we may confuse this picture with Goethe's individuality. It is all the more bewildering because the image is alive and answers questions, and the answers are not only those given in the past, but quite new ones. They are not repetitions of anything that Goethe actually said, but answers he might well have given. It is even possible that this Akasha image of Goethe might write a poem in Goethe's own style. The Akasha pictures are real, living pictures. Strange as these facts may seem, they are none the less facts.

LIFE OF THE SOUL IN KAMALOKA

How does man spend the period between death and a new birth? To call death the elder brother of sleep is not unjustified, for between sleep and death there is a certain relationship; but even so there is a great, decisive difference between them. Let us consider what happens to a man from the moment when he falls asleep to the moment when he wakes up. This stretch of time appears to us as a kind of unconsciousness; only a few memories of the dream-state, sometimes confused and sometimes fairly clear, emerge from it. If we want to understand sleep properly, we must recall the separate members of the human entity.

We have seen that man consists of seven members. Four are fully developed, the fifth only partly so, and of the sixth and seventh only the seed and outline so far exist. Thus we have:

1. The physical body, which we can perceive with our ordinary senses.
2. The etheric body, which permeates the physical body with a delicate luminosity.
3. The astral body.
4. The Ego-body or consciousness body.

This "Ego-body" contains:

5. Spirit-Self, or Manas, partly developed, partly still in embryo.
6. Life-Spirit, or Buddhi.
7. Spirit-Man, or Atma.

These last two are present only as seeds.

In the waking state a man has the first four of these bodies around him in space. The etheric body extends a little beyond the physical body on all sides. The astral body extends about two-and-a-half times the length of the head beyond the physical body, surrounds it like a cloud and fades away as you go from the head downwards. When a man falls asleep, the physical and etheric bodies remain on the bed, united as in the daytime. The astral body loosens its hold, and the astral body and Ego-body raise themselves out of the physical body. Now since all perceptions, concepts and so on are dependent on the astral body, which is now outside the physical body, man loses consciousness in sleep, for in this life he needs the physical brain as an instrument of consciousness; without it he cannot be conscious.

What does the loosened astral body do during the night? A clairvoyant can see that it has a specific task. It does not, as some theosophists will tell you, merely hover above the physical body, inactive, like a passive image; it works continuously on the physical body. During the day the physical body gets tired and used up, and the task of the astral body is to make good this weariness and exhaustion. It renovates the physical body and renews the forces which have been used up during the day. Hence comes the need for sleep, and hence also its refreshing, healing effect. The question of dreams we will deal with later.

When a man dies, things are different. The etheric body then leaves him, as well as the astral body and Ego. These three bodies rise away and for a time remain united. At the moment of death the connection between the astral body and etheric body, on the one hand, and with the physical body, on the other, is broken, particularly in the region of the heart. A sort of light shines forth in the heart, and then the etheric body, the astral body and the Ego can be seen rising up from out of the head.

The actual instant of death brings a remarkable experience: for a brief space of time the man remembers all that has happened to him in the life just ended. His entire life appears before his soul in a moment, like a great tableau. Something like this can happen during life, in rare moments of great shock or anger—for instance a man who is drowning, or falling from a great height, when death seems imminent, may see his whole life before him in this way.

A similar phenomenon is the peculiar tingling feeling we have when a limb "goes to sleep". What happens here is that the etheric body is loosened. If a finger, for example, goes to sleep, a clairvoyant would see a little second finger protruding at the side of the actual finger: this is a part of the etheric body which has got loose. Herein also lies the danger of hypnotism, for the brain then has the same experience as the finger has when it goes to sleep. The clairvoyant can see the loosened etheric body hanging like a pair of bags or sacks on either side of the head. If the hypnotism is repeated, the etheric body will develop an inclination to get loose, and this can be very dangerous. The victims become dreamy, subject to fainting fits, lose their independence, and so on.

A similar loosening of the etheric body occurs when a person is faced with a sudden danger of death. The cause of this similarity is that the etheric body is the bearer of memory; the more strongly developed it is, the stronger a person's faculty of memory will be. While the etheric body is firmly rooted in the physical body, as normally it is, its vibrations cannot act on the brain sufficiently to become conscious, because the physical body with its coarser rhythms conceals them. But in moments of deadly danger the etheric body is loosened, and with its memories it detaches itself from the brain and a man's whole life flashes before his soul. At such moments everything that has been inscribed on the etheric body reappears; hence also the recollection of the whole past life immediately after death. This lasts for some time, until the etheric body separates from the astral body and the Ego.

With most people, the etheric body dissolves gradually into the world-ether. With lowly, uneducated people it dissolves slowly; with cultivated people it dissolves quickly; with disciples or pupils it dissolves slowly again, and the higher a man's development, the slower the process becomes, until finally a stage is reached when the etheric body dissolves no longer.

In the case of ordinary men, then, we have two corpses, of the physical and etheric bodies; we are left with the astral body and the Ego. If we are to understand this condition we must realise that in his earthly life a man's consciousness depends entirely on his senses. Let us think away everything that comes to us through our senses: without our eyes, absolute darkness; without our ears, absolute silence; and no feeling of heat or cold without the appropriate senses. If we can clearly envisage what will remain when we are parted from all our physical organs, from everything that normally fills our daytime consciousness and enlivens the soul, from everything for which we have to be grateful to the body all day long, we shall begin to form some conception of what the condition of life is after death, when the two corpses have been laid aside. This condition is called Kamaloka, the place of desires. It is not some region set apart: Kamaloka is where we are, and the spirits of the dead are always hovering around us, but they are inaccessible to our physical senses. What, then, does a dead man feel? To take a simple example, suppose a man eats avidly and enjoys his food. The clairvoyant will see the satisfaction of his desire as a brownish-red thought-form in the upper part of his astral body. Now suppose the man dies: what is left to him is his desire and capacity for enjoyment. To the physical part of a man belongs only the means of enjoyment: thus we need gums and so forth in order to eat. The pleasure and the desire belong to the soul, and they survive after death. But the man no longer has any means of satisfying his desires, for the appropriate organs are absent. And this applies to all kinds of wishes and desires. He may want to look at some beautiful arrangements of colours—but he lacks eyes; or to listen to some harmonious music—but he lacks ears.

How does the soul experience all this after death? The soul is like a wanderer in the desert, suffering from a burning thirst and looking for some spring at which to quench it;

and the soul has to suffer this burning thirst because it has no organ or instrument for satisfying it. It has to feel deprived of everything, so that to call this condition one of burning thirst is very appropriate. This is the essence of Kamaloka. The soul is not tortured from outside, but has to suffer the torment of the desires it still has but cannot satisfy.

Why does the soul have to endure this torment? The reason is that man has to wean himself gradually from these physical wishes and desires, so that the soul may free itself from the Earth, may purify and cleanse itself. When that is achieved, the Kamaloka period comes to an end and man ascends to Devachan.

How does the soul pass through its life in Kamaloka? In Kamaloka a man lives through his whole life again, but backwards. He goes through it, day by day, with all its experiences, events and actions, back from the moment of death to that of birth. What is the point of this? The point is that he has to pause at every event and learn how to wean himself from his dependence on the physical and material. He also relives everything he enjoyed in his earthly life, but in such a way that he has to do without all this; it offers him no satisfaction. And so he gradually learns to disengage himself from physical life. And when he has lived through his life right back to the day of his birth, he can, in the words of the Bible, enter into the "kingdom of Heaven". As Christ says, "Unless ye became as little children, ye cannot enter the kingdom of Heaven." All the Gospel sayings have a deep meaning, and we come to know their depth only by gradually entering into the divine wisdom.

There are some particular moments in Kamaloka which must be singled out as specially important and instructive. Among the various feelings a man can have as part of his ordinary life is the sheer joy of being alive, of living in a physical body. Hence he feels the lack of physical body as one of his worst deprivations. We can thus understand the terrible destiny and the horrible torments which have to be endured by the unfortunates who end their lives through suicide. When death comes naturally, the three bodies separate relatively easily. Even in apoplexy or any other sudden but natural form of death, the separation of these higher members has in fact been prepared for well in advance, and so they separate easily and the sense of loss of the physical body is only slight. But when the separation is as sudden and violent as it is with the suicide, whose whole organism is still healthy and firmly bound together, then immediately after death he feels the loss of the physical body very keenly and this causes terrible pains. This is a ghastly fate: the suicide feels as though he had been plucked out of himself, and he begins a fearful search for the physical body of which he was so suddenly deprived. Nothing else bears comparison with this. You may retort that the suicide who is weary of life no longer has any interest in it; otherwise he would not have killed himself. But that is a delusion, for it is precisely the suicide who wants too much from life. Because it has ceased to satisfy his desire for pleasure, or perhaps because some change of circumstances has involved him in a loss, he takes refuge in death. And that is why his feeling of deprivation when he finds himself without a body is unspeakably severe.

But Kamaloka is not so hard for everyone. If a man has been less dependent on material pleasures, he naturally finds the loss of his body easier to endure. Even he, however, has to shake himself free from his physical life, for there is a further meaning in Kamaloka. During his life a man does not merely do things which yield pleasure; he lives also in the company of other men and other creatures. Consciously or unconsciously, intentionally or unintentionally, he causes pleasure and pain, joy and sorrow, to animals and men. All such occasions he will encounter again as he lives through the Kamaloka period; he returns to the place and moment when he was the cause of pain to another being. At that time he made someone else feel pain; now he has to suffer the same pain in his own soul. All the torment I ever caused to other beings I now have to live through in my own soul.

I enter into the person or the animal and come to know what the other being was made to suffer through me; now I have to suffer all these pains and torments myself. There is no way of avoiding it. All this is part of the process of freeing oneself—not from the working of karma, but from earthly things. A vivisectionist has a particularly terrible life in Kamaloka.

It is not for a theosophist to criticise what goes on in the world around him, but he can well understand how it is that modern men have come to actions of this kind. In the Middle Ages no one would have ever dreamt of destroying life in order to understand it, and in ancient times any doctor would have looked on this as the height of madness. In the Middle Ages a number of people were still clairvoyant; doctors could see into a man and could discern any injury or defect in his physical body. So it was with Paracelsus, for example. But the material culture of modern times had to come, and with it a loss of clairvoyance. We see this particularly in our scientists and doctors; and vivisection is a result of it. In this way we can come to understand it, but we should never excuse or justify it. The consequences of a life which has been the cause of pain to others are bound to follow, and after death the vivisectionist has to endure exactly the same pains that he inflicted on animals. His soul is drawn into every pain he caused. It is no use saying that to inflict pain was not his intention, or that he did it for the sake of science or that his purpose was good. The law of spiritual life is inflexible.

How long does a man remain in Kamaloka? For about one-third of the length of his past life. If for instance he has lived for seventy-five years, his time in Kamaloka will be twenty-five years. And what happens then? The astral bodies of people vary widely in colour and form. The astral body of a primitive kind of man is permeated with all kinds of shapes and lower desires: its background colour is a reddish-grey, with rays of the same colour emanating from it; in its contours it is no different from that of certain animals. With a highly educated man, or an idealist such as Schiller or a saint such as St. Francis of Assisi, things are quite different. They denied themselves many things; they ennobled their desires and so forth. The more a man uses his Ego to work on himself, the more rays will you see spreading out from the bluish sphere which is his Ego-centre. These rays indicate the forces by means of which a man gains power over his astral body. Hence one can say that a man has two astral bodies: one part has remained as it was, with its animal impulses; the other results from his own work upon it.

When a man has lived through his time in Kamaloka, he will be ready to raise the higher part of his astral body, the outcome of his own endeavours, and to leave the lower part behind. With savages and uncultivated people, a large part of the lower astral body remains behind; with more highly developed people there is much less. When for example a Francis of Assisi dies, very little will be left behind; a powerful higher astral body will go with him, for he will have worked greatly on himself. The remaining part is the third human corpse, consisting of the lower impulses and desires which have not been transmuted. This corpse continues to hover about in astral space, and may be a source of many dangerous influences.

This, too, is a body which can manifest in spiritualistic séances. It often survives for a long time, and may come to speak through a medium. People then begin to believe that it is the dead man speaking, when it is only his astral corpse. The corpse retains its lower impulses and habits in a kind of husk; it can even answer questions and give information, and can speak with just as much sense as the "lower man" used to display. All sorts of confusions may then arise, and a striking example of this is the pamphlet written by the spiritualist, Langsdorf, in which he professes to have had communication with H. P. Blavatsky. To Langsdorf the idea of reincarnation is like a red rag to a bull; there is nothing he would not do to refute this doctrine. He hates H.P.B. because she taught this doctrine and spread it abroad. In his pamphlet he purports to be quoting H.P.B. as having told him not only that the doctrine of reincarnation was false but that she was very sorry ever to have taught it. This may indeed be all correct—except that Langsdorf was not questioning and quoting the real H.P.B. but her astral corpse. It is quite understandable that her lower astral body should answer in this way if we remember that during her early period, in her *Isis Unveiled*, she really did reject and oppose the idea of reincarnation. She herself came to know better, but her error clung to her astral husk.

This third corpse, the astral husk, gradually dissolves, and it is important that it should have dissolved completely before a man returns to a new incarnation. In most cases this duly happens, but in exceptional cases a man may reincarnate quickly, before his astral corpse has dissolved. He has difficulties to face if, when he is about to reincarnate, he finds his own astral corpse still in existence, containing everything that had remained imperfect in his former life.

DEVACHAN

We have seen how at his death a man leaves behind him the corpse, first of his physical body, then of his etheric body and finally of his lower astral body. What is then left when he has shed these three bodies? The memory-picture which comes before the soul at death vanishes at the moment when the etheric body takes leave of the astral. It sinks into the unconscious, so to speak, and ceases to have any significance for the soul as an immediate impression. But although the picture itself vanishes, something important, something that may be called its fruit, survives. The total harvest of the last life remains like a concentrated essence of forces in the higher astral body and rests there.

But a man has often gone through all this in the past. At each death, at the end of each incarnation, this memory-picture has appeared before his soul and left behind what I have called a concentrated essence of forces. So with each life a picture is added. After his first incarnation a man had his first memory-picture when he died; then came the second, richer than the first, and so on. The sum-total of these pictures produces a kind of new element in man. Before his first death a man consists of four bodies, but when he dies for the first time he takes the first memory-picture with him. Thus on reincarnating for the first time he has not only his four bodies but also this product of his former life. This is the "causal" body. So now he has five bodies: physical, etheric, astral, ego and causal. Once this causal body has made its appearance, it remains, though it was first constituted from the products of previous lives. Now we can understand the difference between individuals. Some of them have lived through many lives and so have added many pages to their Book of Life. They have developed to a high level and possess a rich causal body. Others have been through only a few lives; hence they have gathered fewer fruits and have a less developed causal body.

What is the purpose of man's repeated appearance on Earth? If there were no connection between the various incarnations, the whole process would of course be senseless, but that is not how it goes. Think how different life was for a man who was incarnated a few centuries after Christ, compared with the conditions he will find when he reincarnates today. Nowadays a child's life between the sixth and fourteenth years is taken up with acquiring knowledge: reading, writing, and so on. Opportunities for the cultivation and development of human personality are very different from what they were in the past. A man's incarnations are ordered in such a way that he returns to the Earth only when he will find quite new conditions and possibilities of development, and after a few centuries they will always be there. Think how quickly the Earth is developing in every respect: only a few thousand years ago this region was covered with primeval forests, full of wild beasts. Men lived in caves, wore animal skins and had only the most primitive knowledge of how to light a fire or make tools. How different it all is today! We can see how the face of the Earth has been transformed in a relatively short time. A man who lived in the days of the ancient Germanic people had a picture of the world quite different from the picture which prevails today among people who learn to read and write. As the Earth changes, man learns quite new things and makes them his own.

What is the usual period between two incarnations and on what does it depend? The following considerations will give us the answer and we shall see how the changing conditions of the Earth come into it.

In the course of time certain Beings have been particularly revered. For example, in Persia in 3000 B.C. the Twins (Gemini) were specially revered; between 3000 B.C. and 800 B.C. the sacred Bull Apis (Taurus) was revered in Egypt and the Mithras Bull in Asia Minor. After 800 B.C. another

Being came into the foreground and the Ram or Lamb (Aries) was revered. So arose the legend of Jason, who went to fetch the Golden Fleece from the sacred Ram in Asia beyond the sea. The lamb was so highly revered that in due time Christ called Himself the "Lamb of God", and the first Christian symbol was not the Cross with the Saviour hanging on it, but the Cross together with the Lamb.

This means that there were three successive periods of civilisation, each associated with important happenings in the heavens. The Sun takes his course in the sky along a particular path, the Ecliptic, and at the beginning of Spring in a given epoch the Sun rises at a definite point in the Zodiac. So in the year 3000 B.C. the Sun rose in Spring in the constellation of the Bull; before that in the constellation of the Twins, and about 800 B.C. in the constellation of the Ram. This vernal point moves slowly backwards round the Zodiac year by year, taking 2,160 years to pass from one constellation to the next, and people chose as the symbol of their reverence the heavenly sign in which the vernal Sun appeared. If today we were able to understand the powerful feelings and the exalted states of mind which the ancients experienced as the Sun passed on into a new constellation, we should understand also the significance of the moment when the Sun entered the sign of Pisces. But for the materialism of our time no such understanding is possible.

What was it, then, that people saw in this process? The ancients saw it as an embodiment of the forces of nature. In Winter these forces were asleep, but in Spring they were recalled to life by the Sun. Hence the constellation in which the Sun appeared in Spring symbolised these reawakening forces; it gave new strength to the Sun and was felt to be worthy of particular reverence. The ancients knew that with this movement of the Sun round the Zodiac something important was connected, for it meant that the Sun's rays fell on the Earth under quite different conditions as time went on. And indeed the period of 2,160 years does signify a complete change in the conditions of life on Earth. And this is the length of time spent in Devachan between death and a new birth. Occultism has always recognised these 2,160 years as a period during which conditions on Earth change sufficiently for a man to reappear there in order to gain new experience.

We must remember, however, that during this period a person is generally born twice, once as a man and once as a woman, so that on average the interval between two incarnations is in fact about 1,000 years. It is not true that there is a change from male to female at every seventh incarnation. The experiences of the soul are obviously very different in a male incarnation from those it encounters in a female incarnation. Hence the general rule is that a soul appears once as a man and once as a woman during this period of 2,160 years. It will then have had all the experiences available to it under the conditions of that period; and the person will have had the possibility and opportunity to add a new page to his Book of Life. These radical changes in the conditions on Earth provide a schooling for the soul. That is the purpose of reincarnation.

A man takes with him into Devachan his causal body and the purified, ennobled parts of his astral and etheric bodies; these belong to him permanently and he never loses them. At a particular moment, just after he has laid aside his astral corpse, he stands face to face with himself as if he were looking at himself from the outside. That is the moment when he enters Devachan.

Devachan has four divisions:

1. The continents
2. The rivers and oceans
3. The airy region; etheric space
4. The region of spiritual archetypes

In the first division everything is seen as though in a photographic negative. Everything physical that has ever existed on this Earth, whether as mineral, plant or animal, and everything physical that still exists, appears as a negative. And if you see yourself in this negative form, as one among all the others, you will be in Devachan. What is the point of seeing yourself in this way?

You do not see yourself once only, but by degrees you come to see yourself as you were in former lives, and this has a deep purpose. Goethe says: "The eye is formed by the light for the light." He means that light is the creator of the eye, and this is perfectly true. We see how true it is if we observe how the eye degenerates in the absence of light. For example, in Kentucky certain creatures went to live in caves; the caves were dark and so the creatures did not need eyes. Gradually they lost the light of the eyes, and their eyes atrophied. The vital fluids which had formerly nourished their eyes were diverted to another organ which was now more useful for them. These creatures, then, lost their sight because their whole world was without light: the absence of light destroyed their power of sight. Thus if there were no light, there would be no eyes. The forces which create the eye are in the light, just as the forces which create the ear are in the world of sound. In short, all the organs of the body are built up by the creative forces of the universe. If you ask what has built the brain, the answer is that without thinking there would be no brain. There are mighty laws of nature. Such men as Kepler or Galileo turned their understanding to these laws. Who created the organ of understanding? The wisdom of nature!

Ordinarily a man enters the earthly world with his organs to a certain extent perfected. During the interval since his last incarnation, however, new conditions have arisen, and he has to work upon them with his spirit. In all his experiences there is a creative power. His eyes, and the understanding which he already possesses, were formed in an earlier incarnation. When after death he reaches Devachan, he finds, as we have seen, the picture of his body as it was in his last life, and within him he still carries the fruits of the memory-picture of his last life. It is now possible for him to compare the course of his development in his various lives: what he was like before the experiences of his last life and what he can become when the experiences of this latest life are added to those of the others. Accordingly he forms for himself a picture of a new body, standing one step higher than his previous bodies.

At the first stage in Devachan, therefore, a man corrects his previous life-picture, and out of the fruits of his former lives he prepares the picture of his body for his next incarnation.

At the second stage in Devachan, life pulsates as a reality, as though in rivers and streams. During earthly existence a man has life within him and he cannot perceive it; now he sees it flowing past and he uses it to animate the form he had built up at the first stage.

At the third stage of Devachan, a man is surrounded by all the passions and feelings of his past life, but now they come before him as clouds, thunder and lightning. He sees all this as it were objectively; he learns to understand it, and to observe it as he observes physical things on Earth; and he gathers all his experiences into the life of his soul. By dint of seeing these pictures of the life of soul he is able to incorporate their particular qualities, and thus he endows with soul the body he had formed at the first stage.

That is the purpose of Devachan. A man has to advance a stage further there, so he himself prepares the image of his body for his next incarnation. That is one of his tasks in Devachan; but he has many others also. He is by no means concerned only with himself. Everything he does is done in full consciousness. He lives consciously in Devachan, and statements to the contrary in theosophical books are false. How is this to be understood? When a man is asleep, his astral body leaves the physical and etheric bodies, and consciousness leaves him also. But that is true only while the astral body is engaged on its usual task of repairing and restoring harmony to the weary and worked out physical body. When a man has died, his astral body no longer has this task to perform, and in proportion as it is released from this task, consciousness awakens. During the man's life his consciousness was darkened and hemmed in by the physical forces of the body and at night he had to work on this physical body. When the forces of the astral body are released after death, its own specific organs immediately emerge. These are the seven lotus-flowers, the Chakrams. Thus at the root of the nose, between the eyebrows, the two-petalled lotus-flower arises. Clairvoyant artists have been aware of this and gave it a symbol in their works: Michaelangelo created his statue of Moses with two little horns. The lotus-flowers are distributed as follows:

The 16-petalled lotus-flower in the region of the larynx;
The 12-petalled lotus-flower in the neighbourhood of the heart;
The 8- or 10-petalled lotus-flower in the region of the stomach;
A 6- and a 4-petalled lotus-flower are to be found lower down.

These astral organs are hardly observable in the ordinary man of today, but if he becomes clairvoyant, or goes into a state of trance, they stand out in shining, living colours, and are in motion. Directly the lotus-flowers are in motion, a man perceives the astral world. But the difference between physical and astral organs is that physical organs are passive and allow everything to act on them from outside. Eye, ear and so on have to wait until light or sound brings them a message. Spiritual organs, on the other hand, are active; they hold objects in their grip. But this activity can awaken only when the forces of the astral body are not otherwise employed; then they stream into the lotus-flowers. Even in Kamaloka, as long as the lower parts of the astral body are still united to the man, the astral organs are dimmed. It is only when the astral corpse has been discarded and nothing remains with the man except what he has acquired as permanent parts of himself—i.e. at the entrance to Devachan

—that these astral sense-organs wake to full activity; and in Devachan man lives with them in a high degree of consciousness.

It is incorrect for theosophical books to say that man is asleep in Devachan; incorrect that he is concerned only with himself, or that relationships begun on Earth are not continued there. On the contrary, a friendship truly founded on spiritual affinity continues with great intensity. The circumstances of physical life on Earth bring about real experiences there. The inwardness of friendship brings nourishment to the communion of spirits in Devachan and enriches it with new patterns; it is precisely this which feeds the soul there. Again, an elevated aesthetic enjoyment of nature is nourishment for the life of the soul in Devachan.

All this is what human beings live on in Devachan. Friendships are as it were the environment with which a man surrounds himself there. Physical conditions all too often cut across these relationships on Earth. In Devachan the way in which two friends are together depends only on the intensity of their friendship. To form such relationships on Earth provides experiences for life in Devachan.

HUMAN TASKS IN THE HIGHER WORLDS

Yesterday we came to know a little about the nature of Devachan; now we have to ask how the bliss of Devachan comes about. Most of the activity there is creative, and though it is difficult to give an idea of the bliss that goes with it, a comparison with something that occurs on Earth will perhaps bring us nearer to it.

Let us observe the feeling that pervades the activity of a being engaged in the creation of another being: for instance, a hen sitting on her eggs. This is really a very appropriate comparison, grotesque though it may sound, for the brooding hen experiences an immense and blissful sense of well-being. Transfer this feeling to the spiritual level and you will have some conception of Devachan.

In the first region, the continental, where everything physical is spread out in negative, but like a vast tableau, a man is under an obligation to create the image of his new body. He does this free of all hindrance, and in so doing feels the bliss of creation.

In the second region, the universal life which under physical conditions is tied up with the forms of man, animal and plant, flows freely like the waters of the sea; and a man sees this flow as something both external and internal. Externally he sees it flow in a reddish-lilac stream from one plant form to another, one animal form to another, all embraced in the unity of life. All forms of spiritual life, for example that of Christian communities, are seen as belonging to the universal flow of life. Hence the first rule for a theosophist, which is to look for the one life in everything, can be truly practised; for the universal life, common to all things, is seen in flow.

In the third region one sees realised in visible form all

the relationships that arise between human beings on the level of the soul. If two people love one another, one sees the love as a real being whose body is love. If you can make a picture of all this for yourselves, you will have some idea of the bliss of Devachan; but anyone who has any knowledge of it will use few words, for the spiritual cannot be rendered in physical language.

But you must not think a man is inactive in Devachan, or is concerned only with himself. He has something else to do there.

The countenance of the Earth, with all its flora and fauna, is continually changing: how different, for instance, must things have been in northern Siberia when the mammoth, still to be found as though frozen alive in the ice-fields, lived there. How different things must have been here, when primeval forest still covered the ground, when wild animals of the torrid zone lived here and a tropical climate prevailed. Who is it that brings all this about? Who changes conditions on the Earth? How is it with the souls and spirits of animals, and with the souls of plants?

If we are talking only of the physical plane, we are quite justified in saying that man has his Ego and his dwelling-place here, and that man is the highest of the beings who live on the Earth. On the astral plane things are quite different. As soon as an Initiate enters that plane, he comes to know a whole range of new beings who are not present on the physical plane, but appear on the astral plane as beings like himself. Among them are the species-souls or group-souls of animals, and one associates with them as one does with other people on the physical plane. On the physical plane animals have only a physical, an etheric and an astral body; they have no Ego there, for their Ego is to be found on the astral plane. Just as your ten fingers have a common soul, all animals of one species have their common soul on the astral plane. The Ego of the species lion, dog, or ant, and so on, is to be found there as a real being. It is as though the Ego hovered in astral space and held the indi-

43

vidual animals on strings like marionettes. Plants also have group-souls of this kind, but their Ego is in Devachan; the "strings" go still higher. And all the minerals, such as gold, diamonds, rocks and so forth, have their group-soul in the upper region of Devachan.

The various beings, then, are ranked in the following way:

	Man	Animal	Plant	Mineral
Upper Devachan	–	–	–	Ego
Lower Devachan	–	–	Ego	Astral body
Astral Plane	–	Ego	Astral body	Etheric body
Physical Plane	Ego	–	–	–
	Astral body	Astral body	–	–
	Etheric body	Etheric body	Etheric body	–
	Physical body	Physical body	Physical body	Physical body

When a man dies, his Ego is to be found together with Egos of the animals, and the work he can be engaged on is similar to that of the Egos of the animals—to produce gradual changes in the animal world. In Lower Devachan he finds the Egos of the plants as his companions, and there he can alter the forms of the plant-world. In this way he can collaborate in the transformation of the Earth. Hence it is man himself who brings about the great changes in the countenance of the Earth, and also the greatly altered scene in which he lives during his next incarnation. But he carries out this work under the leadership and guidance of higher Beings. Thus it is true to say, when we look at the continually changing plant and animal worlds, that this change is the work of the dead. The dead are active in the transformation of flora and fauna, and even in changing the physical form of the solid Earth. Even in the forces of nature we have to see the activity of discarnate human beings; and we know how powerfully these forces can work on the face of the Earth.

All activity, all work, had its beginning at some time long ago. There were as yet no pyramids, not even any tools. Everything existed in the form given to it by gods, or, as materialists would say, by the forces of nature; and man was set into the midst of it all. Now, however, most of our surroundings are the work of man. Thus the Earth is always being transformed by man. This will go on increasingly, and what man cannot accomplish here, he carries out in the period between death and rebirth. Thus our own evolution is tied up with the changes of the whole Earth. The structure and evolution of the Earth are the work of men on higher planes, and the more highly man succeeds in developing himself, the more quickly and perfectly will the transformation of the physical Earth, and of its flora and fauna, advance. The more highly developed a man is, the longer is the time he can spend at work in the higher regions of Devachan. A savage sees little of it. In many stories and legends the human spirit—apparently childish but in reality inspired by lofty powers—has given expression to these facts.

Now how do the forces act which bring man down to a new incarnation? As we saw, there is an interval of about 1,000 years between death and the next incarnation, and during this period the soul is making itself ready for its journey to a new birth. It is exceedingly interesting for a clairvoyant to explore the astral world. He may, for example, observe astral corpses floating about, in process of dissolution. The astral corpse of a highly developed man, who has worked on his lower impulses, will dissolve very quickly, but with undeveloped persons, who have given free rein to their impulses and passions, the process of dissolution goes slowly. Sometimes the earlier astral corpse is not wholly dissolved when its original bearer returns to a new birth, and he will then face a difficult destiny. It can also happen that through special circumstances a man returns soon and finds his astral corpse still present. The corpse is then strongly drawn to him and slips into his new astral body. He does indeed create a new astral body, but the old one combines with it, and he has to drag both of them along throughout his life. And then in bad dreams or visions the old astral body comes before him as a second Ego, playing tricks on him, harassing and tormenting him. This is the false, counterfeit Guardian of the Threshold. An old astral corpse finds it easy to withdraw from a man because it is not firmly united with the other members of his being, and then it appears as a Double, a *Doppelgänger*.

Besides these astral forms, the clairvoyant sees another particularly remarkable set of shapes. They are bell-shaped and shoot through astral space with enormous speed. They are germinal human beings not yet incarnated but striving for incarnation. Time and space hardly matter to these beings because they can move about very easily. They are variously coloured and surrounded by an aura of colour: at one point they are red, at another blue, and a shining yellow ray flashes out from inside them. These germinal human beings have just come from Devachan into astral space. What is happening here?

After a man has taken with him into Devachan his higher astral body, and the causal body made up of the fruits of his former lives, he now has to gather round him new "astral substance" rather as scattered iron filings are brought into order by the pull of a magnet. He collects this astral substance in accordance with the forces within him: the substance collected after a good previous life is different from the substance collected after a bad one. The bell-shaped forms are made up of the causal body, the forces of the earlier astral body and the new astral body. The germinal human being ought not to encounter the old astral body; his task is to build up a new astral body out of undifferentiated astral substance, so that the whole process depends on the man himself. The form and colour of the new astral body are determined by the forces of his previous life: this is a fact to be kept thoroughly well in mind. The reason why the germinal human beings dart about with such enormous speed is that they are searching for parents with suitable characters and family circumstances. Their speed helps them to find the right parents—they can be here at one moment and in America the next.

For the next stage, help is needed. Higher Beings, the

Lipikas, guide the germinal human being to the chosen parents; the "Maharajas" form the etheric body to correspond with the astral form and with the contribution by the parents to the physical body. The clairvoyant can descry astral substance in the passion experienced by the parents during the act of impregnation, and the passional nature of the child is determined by the intensity of the passion felt by the parents. After this, etheric substance shoots in from north, south, east and west, from the heights and from the depths.

Parents who will be exactly right for the germinal human being cannot always be found; all that can be done is to search for the most suitable. Similarly, a physical body cannot always be built so as to match exactly the incoming etheric body. There can never be complete harmony. This is the reason for the discord between soul and body in human beings.

Immediately before incarnation a very important event occurs, parallel to the event which follows the moment of death. Just as immediately after death the whole memory of a man's past life appears like a tableau before his soul, so is a kind of preview of the coming life given to the soul immediately before it incarnates. Not all the details are seen, but the circumstances of the coming life are made evident in broad outline. This is of the utmost importance. It may happen that a person who went through a great deal of suffering and hardship in his previous life receives a shock from the glimpse of the new circumstances and destiny now in prospect, and holds back the soul from complete incarnation. Only a part of the soul then enters the body, and this will result in the birth of an epileptic or an idiot.

At the moment of incarnation, immediately after conception, the yellow thread in the causal body darkens and disappears. It persists through all stages only in Initiates.

We must not imagine that the higher members of a man's being unite completely with the embryo from the beginning. The causal body is the first to be active, for it works

47

on the earliest formation of the physical body.

Development goes on after birth by stages, in the most varied ways; specially important for education is the period from the seventh to the fourteenth year. We shall see tomorrow how Theosophy bears on these problems of education, which point to an important chapter in human evolution.

THE UPBRINGING OF CHILDREN.
KARMA

The grasp of life given by Theosophy is in the highest sense practical. The light it throws on questions of education will be deeply useful to humanity long before people are clairvoyant, and long before a person attains to direct vision he can convince himself that in Theosophy the truth about life is to be found.

Once he is born, the human being enters on a new life, and his various bodies develop in different ways and at different times. The educator should always bear this in mind. The period from the first to the seventh year is very different from the second seven-year period from the seventh to the fifteenth or sixteenth year—earlier with girls, later with boys. Then there is a change again after the six-teenth year, or shall we say after puberty. We can properly understand how a human being grows to maturity only if we keep before our eyes the different ways in which the various members of his being develop.

From birth to the seventh year it is really only the physical body that parents and educators have to consider. At birth the physical body is released into its environment; before birth it is part of the maternal organism. During the whole period of pregnancy the life of the mother and of the human embryo are intermingled. The physical body of the mother surrounds the physical body of the child, so that the outer world has no access to the child. At birth, things change; only then can the child receive impressions from other beings in the physical world. But the child's etheric and astral bodies are still not open to the external world; up to the seventh year, indeed, the external world cannot influence them, for they are inwardly absorbed in building up the physical body. At about the seventh year the etheric body begins to be free to receive impressions from outside, and it can then be influenced. But from the seventh to the fourteenth year no attempt should be made to influence the astral body, or its inward activity will be disturbed. During the first seven years it is best to leave the etheric and astral bodies quite unmolested and to rely on everything happening of its own accord.

The best way to influence the child during his first seven years is through the development of his sense-organs. All the impressions they receive from the outer world are significant, and everything a child sees or hears affects him in terms of his sense-organs. The sense-organs, however, are not influenced by lesson-books or verbal teaching, but by means of example and imitation. The most important thing during the first seven years is to nourish a child's sense-organs. He will see with his eyes how people round him are behaving. Aristotle was quite right in saying that man is the most imitative of all creatures; and this is particularly true during the first seven years. Hence during these years we must try to influence a child's senses, to draw them out so that they become active on their own account. That is why it is such a mistake to give a child one of those "beautiful" dolls; they hinder him from setting his own inner powers to work. A normal child will reject the doll and be much happier with a piece of wood, or with anything which gives his imagination a chance to be active.

No particular method of teaching is needed for the etheric and astral bodies, but it is extremely important that the subtler influences which pass over to them unconsciously from their environment should be favourable. It is very important that during these early years a child should be surrounded by noble-minded, generous-hearted and affectionate people with good thoughts, for these stamp themselves on the child's inner life. Example, therefore, in thought and in feeling is the best means of education at this stage. It is not what we say but what we *are* that influences a child during his first seven years. Because of the extreme sensitivity of the inner members of a child's being, his surroundings should be kept free from all impure, immoral thoughts and feelings.

From the seventh to the fourteenth, fifteenth or sixteenth year—that is, until puberty—the etheric body goes through a liberation, just as the physical body is thrown open to its environment at birth. During this period, then, we must direct our efforts to the etheric body, the vehicle of memory, of lasting habits, of temperament and inclinations and enduring desires. Accordingly, when the etheric body is set free we must take every care to develop these features; we must influence a child's habits, his memory, everything which will give his character a firm foundation. The child will grow up like a will-o'-the-wisp if care is not taken to imbue his character with certain lasting habits, so that with their aid he will stand firm against the storms of life. This, too, is the time for exercising his memory; memorising is more difficult after this age. It is at this time also that a feeling for art awakens, particularly for the art of music, so closely associated with the vibrations of the etheric body. If any musical talent exists, this is when we should do all we can to encourage it. This again is the time for stories and parables; it is wrong to try to develop critical faculties so early. Our age sins greatly in this respect. Care must be taken to see that the child learns as much as possible through stories and analogies; we must store his memory with them and must see to it that his power of comparison is exercised on concepts drawn from the sense-world. We must bring before him examples taken from the lives of the great men of history, but there must be no talk of "this is good" or "this is bad", for that would make a demand on his judgment. We can hardly place too many such pictures or examples before the child; these are the things which act on the etheric body. This, too, is the age when stories and fairy tales, which represent human life in the form of pictures, have a powerful effect. All this makes the etheric body supple and plastic and provides it with lasting impressions. How grateful Goethe must have been to his mother for telling him so many fairy stories at this age!

The later the power of critical judgment is aroused in a child, the better. But children ask "why?" We should answer such questions not with abstract explanations but through examples and images. And how infinitely important it is to find the right ones! If a child asks questions about life and death, and the changes that accompany them, we can use the example of the caterpillar and the chrysalis, and explain how the butterfly arises from the chrysalis to a new life. Everywhere in nature we can find such comparisons, relevant to the highest questions. But quite specially important for the child of this age is *authority*. It must not be an enforced authority—the teacher must gain his authority quite naturally, so that the child will believe before it has knowledge to go on. Theosophical education demands of the teacher not only intellectual knowledge, not only educational principles and insights; it demands that the type of people chosen to be teachers must be those whose natural gifts show promise of their becoming "an authority". Does this seem too much to ask? Surely we cannot fail to get such teachers, since the future of mankind depends on it. Here a great cultural task for Theosophy opens up.

When the child enters the third period of seven years, the age of puberty, the astral body is liberated; on it depends the power of judgment and criticism and the capacity for entering into direct relationships with other human beings. A young person's feelings towards the world in general develop in company with his feelings towards other people, and now he is at last mature enough for real understanding. As the astral body is liberated, so is the personality, and so personal judgment has to be developed. Nowadays young people are expected to offer criticism much too early. Seventeen-year-old critics can be found in abundance, and many of the people who write and pass judgments are quite immature. You have to be twenty-two or twenty-four before you can offer a sound judgment of your own; before then it is quite impossible. From the fourteenth to the twenty-fourth year, when everything around him can teach a person something, is the best time for learning from the world. That is the way to grow up into full maturity.

These are the great basic principles of education; count-less details can be deduced from them. The Theosophical Society is to publish a book for teachers and mothers which will show how from birth to the seventh year the essential thing is *example*; from the seventh to the fourteenth year, *authority*; from the fourteenth to the twenty-first year the training of independent *judgment*.

This is one example of how Theosophy seeks to lay hold of practical life through all its stages.

Another example of practical Theosophy can be drawn from a study of the great law of karma: a law which really makes life comprehensible for the first time. The law of karma is not mere theory, or something that merely satisfies our curiosity. No, it gives us strength and confidence at every stage in life, and makes intelligible much that would otherwise be unintelligible.

First of all, the law of karma answers the great human question: why are children born into such widely differing conditions? For instance, we see one child born to wealth, perhaps endowed also with great talents and surrounded by the most loving care. And we see another child born to poverty and misery, perhaps with few talents or abilities, and so apparently predestined to failure—or a child may have great abilities but no chance to develop them. These are serious problems, and only Theosophy gives an answer to them. If we are to face life with strength and hope we must find an answer. How then does the law of karma answer these riddles?

We have seen that a man passes through repeated lives on Earth, and that when a child is born, it is not for the first time: he has been on Earth many times before. Now in the external world the rule of cause and effect prevails, as everyone recognises, and it is this great natural law of cause and effect which we see, carried over into the spiritual realm, as the law of karma.

How does the law work in the external world? Take a metal ball, heat it and put it on a wooden board. It will burn a hole in the wood. Take another ball, heat it but throw it into water before you put it on the board, and then it will not burn a hole. The fact that the ball was thrown into the water is significant for its later behaviour. The ball goes through a sort of experience, and its behaviour will vary accordingly. Thus the effect depends on the cause. This is an example from the inanimate world, but the same law holds everywhere. Animals gradually lose their eyesight if they go to live in dark caves. Now suppose that in a later generation such an animal were able to reflect: why have I no eyes? It would have to conclude that the cause of its fate was that its ancestors had gone to live in caves. Thus an earlier experience shapes a later destiny, and so the rule of cause and effect holds.

The higher we move in the scale of nature towards man, the more individual does destiny become. Animals have a group-soul, and the destiny of a group of animals is bound up with the group-soul. A man has his own Ego, and the individual Ego undergoes its destiny just as the group-soul of animals does. A whole species of animal may change over the generations, but with man it is the individual Ego that changes from one life to another. Cause and effect go on working from life to life: what I experience today has its cause in a previous life, and what I do today shapes my destiny in my next life. The cause of different circumstances at birth is not to be found in this life; nothing immediate is responsible for it. The cause lies in earlier lives. In a previous life a man has prepared his present destiny.

Surely, you might say, it is just this that must depress a man and rob him of all hope. But in fact the law of karma is the most consoling law there is. Just as it is true that nothing exists without a cause, so it is equally true that nothing existing remains without its effects. I may be born in poverty and misery; my abilities may be very limited; yet whatever I do must produce its effect, and whatever I accomplish now, by way of industry or moral activity, will certainly have its effect in later lives. If it depresses me to think that I have deserved my present destiny, it may equally cheer me to know that I can frame my future destiny myself. Anyone who really takes this law into his thinking and feeling will soon realise what a sense of power and of security he has gained. We do not have to understand the law in all its details; that becomes possible only at the higher stages of clairvoyant knowledge. Much more important is it that we should look at the world in the light of this law and live in accordance with it. If we do this conscientiously over a period of years, the law will of its own accord become part of our feelings. We verify the truth of the law by applying it.

At this point all sorts of objections may arise. Someone may say: "Then we should certainly become sheer fatalists! If we are responsible for whatever happens to us and cannot change it, the best thing is to do nothing. If I am lazy, that is my karma." Or perhaps someone will say: "The law of karma says we can bring about favourable consequences in our next life. I will start being really good in a later life; for the moment I will enjoy myself. I have plenty of time; I shall be returning to Earth and I will make a start then." Someone else says: "I shall not help anyone any more, for if he is poor and wretched and I help him I shall be interfering with his karma. He has earned his suffering; he must look after changing his karma by his own efforts."

All these objections reveal a gross misunderstanding. The law of karma says that all the good I may have done in this life will have its effect, and so will everything bad. Thus in our Book of Life there is a kind of account-sheet, with debit and credit sides, and the balance can be drawn at any moment. If I close the account and draw the balance, that will show my destiny. At first this seems to be a hard, unbending law, but it is not so. A true comparison with the ledger would run as follows: each new transaction alters the balance and each new action alters the destiny.

After all, a merchant does not say that since every new transaction upsets his balance, he can do nothing about it. Just as the merchant is not hindered by his ledger from doing new business, so in life a man is not hindered from making a new entry in his Book of Life. And if the merchant got into difficulties and asked a friend to lend him a thousand marks to help him to recover, it would be nonsense if his friend replied that he really couldn't do anything because it would mean interfering with the state of his friend's account-book. In the same way it would be nonsense if I refused to help another man in order not to come into conflict with the law of karma. However firmly I believe in the law of karma, there is nothing to prevent me from relieving any misery and poverty. On the contrary, if I did not believe in the law, I might doubt whether my help would have any effect: as it is, I know that my help will have a good effect. It is this aspect of karma which can console us and give us energy for action. We ought to think of the law of karma not so much in its relation to the past as in its bearing on the future. We may indeed look back on the past and resolve to bear its karma, but above all we should be positively active in laying a foundation for the future.

Christian clergymen often raise the objection: "Your Theosophy is not Christian, for it ascribes everything to self-redemption. You say a man must work out his own karma quite alone. If he can do this, what place is there for Christ Jesus, who suffered for all mankind? The theosophist says he needs no help from anyone."

All this indicates a misunderstanding on both sides. Our critics do not realise that free-will is not restricted by the law of karma. The theosophist, on his side, needs to see clearly that because he believes in karma he does not depend entirely on self-help and self-development; he must recognise that he can be helped by others. And then a true recon-

56

ciliation between the law of karma and the central fact of Christianity will not be hard to find. This harmony has always existed; the law of karma has always been known to esoteric Christianity.

Let us imagine two people: one is in distress because of his karma, the other helps him because he has the power to do so, and in this way the karma of the former is improved. Does this exclude the law? On the contrary, it confirms it. It is precisely the working of the law of karma which makes the help effective.

If someone has more power than this, he may be able to help two or three or four others if they are in need. Someone still more powerful may be able to help hundreds or thousands and influence their karma for the better. And if he is as powerful as Christianity represents Christ to be, he may help the whole of humanity just at a time when it is in special need of help. But that does not make the law of karma ineffective; on the contrary, Christ's deed on Earth is effective precisely because the law of karma can be built upon.

The Redeemer knows that by the law of karma His work of redemption will be available for everyone. Indeed, He accomplished that deed in reliance on the law of karma, as a cause of glorious results in the future, as a seed for a later harvest and as a source of help for anyone who allows the blessings of redemption to act upon him. Christ's deed is conceivable only because of the law of karma; the testament of Christ is in fact the teaching of karma and reincarnation. This does not mean that each one must bear the consequence of his own actions, but that the consequences must be borne by someone, no matter whom. If a theosophist maintains that he cannot understand the unique deed of Christ having been accomplished once only for all mankind, this means that he does not understand karma. The same is true of any priest who declares that karma interferes with the doctrine of redemption. The reason why Christianity has hitherto failed to emphasise the law of karma and the idea of reincarnation is bound up with the whole question of human evolution and will be dealt with later.

The world does not consist of single "I's", each one isolated from the rest; the world is really one great unity and brotherhood. And just as in physical life a brother or friend can intervene to help another, so does this hold good in a much deeper sense in the spiritual world.

WORKINGS OF THE LAW OF KARMA IN HUMAN LIFE

Today I want to speak about the workings of the law of karma through individual human lives. Any such explanation is bound to be incomplete, for I shall not be putting before you any speculations or theories. I shall limit myself, as occultism always should, to facts and experiences. I shall therefore tell you of a karmic influence of one kind or another only when I have observed a person in that particular situation. In speaking of karmic relationships I shall draw only on real experiences.

We touched yesterday on the fact that for most people the really burning question is: How does our destiny come about and why are we born with talents and circumstances that vary so widely? In order to understand these karmic relationships, we shall have to look back again at what has been said about man's four bodies—the physical, the etheric, the astral, and within them the Ego-body, in which the higher part of the human being is enclosed. In considering karmic relationships we shall be concerned chiefly with how causes and effects are connected with these different bodies.

Let us consider first the physical body, in so far as it bears on the law of karma. All our actions take place in the physical world; if we are to cause anyone pleasure or pain we have to be—of course not literally—in the same place as he is. What we do results from the movements of our physical body and on everything connected with it. Our external destiny in a later life depends upon what we do in this physical life. This external destiny is, as it were, the environment into which we are born. Anyone who has done bad deeds prepares for himself a bad environment, and vice versa. That is the first important karmic law: what we did in a former life determines our external destiny.

There is a second fundamental law. If we look at the way a man develops, we see that in the course of his life he learns an extraordinary amount. He absorbs concepts, ideas, experiences, feelings, and all this produces great changes in him. Think of yourselves as you were a few years ago before you knew anything about Theosophy; think of the new ideas you have acquired and how they have changed your life. All this has produced a corresponding change in the astral body, for it is the most subtle and delicate and responds most quickly to change.

Temperament, character and inclinations change much more slowly. A hot-tempered child, for example, changes very slowly. Temperament, character and inclinations often persist all through life. Ideas and experiences change quickly; it is just the opposite with temperament, character and inclinations. These attributes are very tenacious; they do change, but slowly. Their relation to quickly changing ideas is somewhat like the relation of the hour-hand of a clock to the quick-moving minute-hand. This is because they depend on the etheric body, which consists of substance much less open to change than is the substance of the astral body. Slowest of all to change is the physical body. It is laid down once for all, so to speak, and retains more or less the same character throughout life. We shall see later how the Initiate can work upon his etheric body and can change even his physical body. For the moment we must consider how all this extends beyond a single life.

The ideas, feelings and so on which transform the astral body during a long life will produce a marked change in the etheric body only in the next life. Thus if someone wants to be born in his next life with good habits and inclinations, he must try to prepare these as much as possible in his astral body. If he makes the effort to do good, he will be born in his next life with the tendency to do good and that will be a characteristic of his etheric body. If he wants to be born with a good memory, he must exercise his memory as much as he can; he must practise looking back over the separate years of his life and over his life as a whole. In this way he will engender in his astral body something which will become a characteristic of his etheric body in his next life—the foundation for a good memory. A man who simply hurries through the world will find in his next life that he cannot stick at anything. But if anyone lives in intimate sympathy with a particular environment, he will be born with a special predilection for everything that reminds him of it.

We can trace the various temperaments, also, back to a previous life, for they are qualities of the etheric body.

The choleric man has a strong will, is bold, courageous, with an urge to action. Alexander the Great, Hannibal, Caesar, Napoleon, for example, were cholerics. This type of character shows itself even in childhood, and a child with this temperament will take the lead in childhood games.

The melancholic man is very much occupied with himself and hence is apt to keep himself to himself. He does a lot of thinking, particularly about the way in which his environment affects him. He withdraws into himself, tends to be suspicious. This temperament, too, is apparent in childhood: a child of this type does not like to display his toys; he is afraid something will be taken away from him and would like to keep everything under lock and key.

The phlegmatic man has no real interest in anything; he is dreamy, inactive, lazy, and seeks sensuous enjoyment.

The sanguine man, on the other hand, gets easily interested in anything but he does not stick to it; his interest quickly fades; he is continually changing his hobbies.

These are the four basic types. Generally a man is a mixture of all four, but we can usually discover the fundamental one. These four temperaments express themselves in the etheric body, and so there are four main types of etheric body. They have differing currents and movements, and these impart a particular basic colour to the astral body. This does not depend on the astral body; it only reveals itself there.

The melancholic temperament is karmically determined if a man in his previous life was compelled to lead a narrow, restricted existence and to be much alone; if he was always preoccupied only with himself and unable to take much interest in anything else. If, however, a man has learnt a great deal from experience but has also had something of a hard struggle, if he has encountered many things and has not merely looked on at them, he will become a choleric. If, again, he has had a pleasant life without much struggle or toil, or if he saw and passed by many things, but only as an onlooker, all this will work karmically into the etheric body of his next life: he will become a phlegmatic or a sanguine type.

From this we can see how we can work for our next life: and in occult schools this is done with conscious intention. In former times it was done more often than it is today because of the changes in human evolution. Five thousand years ago the occult teacher had a quite different task. He had to concern himself with people in groups; human beings had not reached the stage where each man has to take responsibility for himself. The deliberate purpose was to enable whole classes and groups of people to work together harmoniously in their next lives. But human beings are becoming more and more individual and independent; the occult teacher can no longer use anyone as a means to an end but has to treat everyone as an end in himself, and to help him to develop as far as is possible for him. In the oldest civilisations, in India for example, the entire population was divided into four castes, and the training given was intended to fit everyone for a particular caste in the next life. The development of human beings, together with the picture of the world they were to have, was deliberately planned for thousands of years ahead, and it was this that gave occult leaders their great power.

How, then, should we try to influence our etheric body for the next life? Everything done to develop the etheric body produces a result, however slowly, and education can take pains to instil quite specific habits. Whatever the etheric body acquires during one life comes to expression in the physical body in the next life. All the habits and inclinations of the present etheric body will create a predisposition to good or bad health. Good habits will produce good health; bad ones will create a tendency to some specific illness in the next life. A strong determination to rid oneself of a bad habit will work down into the physical body and produce a tendency to good health. How a disposition to infectious diseases arises in the physical body has been particularly well observed. Whether we actually get a disease will depend on what we do; but whether we are specially liable to contract it is the result of the inclinations we had in a previous life. Infectious diseases, strangely enough, can be traced back to a highly developed selfish acquisitiveness in a previous life.

If we want really to understand health and illness, we must bear in mind how complicated the circumstances are. Illness need not be a matter of individual karma only; the karma of a whole people has to be taken into account.

An interesting example of how things in the spiritual life are inter-related can be seen in the migration of the Huns and Mongols who poured from Asia into the West. The Mongols were stragglers of the Atlanteans. While the Indians, the Germanic and other peoples were progressing, the Mongols had remained behind. Just as the animals have separated off from the evolutionary path of mankind, so have certain lower peoples and races fallen behind. The Mongols were Atlanteans whose physical development had taken a downward course. In the astral bodies of such decadent people an abundance of decaying astral substance can be seen. When the Mongols fell upon the Germans and other Central European peoples, they created a wave of fear and panic. These emotions belong to the astral body, and under such conditions decaying astral substances will flourish. Thus the astral bodies of Europeans became infected and in later generations the infection came out in the physical body, affecting not merely individuals but whole groups of peoples. It emerged as leprosy, that terrible disease which wrought such devastation in the Middle Ages. It was the physical consequence of an influence on the astral body.

Philology will not help you in finding evidence for this, because it knows nothing of astral influences. But you will at least find some evidence for the descent of the Mongols from the Atlanteans in the names: thus Attila, the leader of the Huns, is called in the Nordic language Atli—meaning someone descended from the Atlanteans.

This then is how diseases affecting whole peoples have originated, and in ancient times some knowledge of it survived. The Bible has a true saying, very often misunderstood, when it speaks of God visiting the sins of the fathers on the children, even to the third and fourth generations. This does not refer to the successive incarnations of individuals, but to a karma affecting whole generations. We have to take the saying literally, as indeed many such statements have to be taken more literally than is usually thought.

The fact is that we must first learn to read the religious sources properly. In ancient times simple-minded people took them literally. As people became more sophisticated, this way of reading became increasingly rare. Then the clever liberal theologians began to expound the sources, each in his own way; and this meant that many passages were not expounded but undermined. Then there was a third stage: that of the people who took everything—old myths and legends and even the life of Christ—as a series of symbols. All this depends on the ingenuity of individuals; some will always be cleverer at it than others. But there is also a fourth stage: that of the occultist, who can once more understand everything literally because through his spiritual knowledge he can see how things are interconnected.

From what has been said you will realise that habits and feelings, which first belong to the spiritual life, can later express themselves in physical life. There is an important principle here: if care is taken to inculcate good habits, not only will the moral life of subsequent generations be improved, but also the health of a whole people, and vice versa. This is then their collective karma.

There is a form of illness, very widespread today, which was hardly known a hundred years ago—nerves or neuroticism—not because it was unrecognised, but because it was so uncommon. This characteristic illness springs from the materialistic outlook of the eighteenth century. Without that, the illness would never have appeared. The occult teacher knows that if this materialism were to continue for a few decades more, it would have a devastating effect on the general health of mankind. If these materialistic habits of thought were to remain unchecked, people would not only be nervous in the ordinary sense but children would be born trembling; they would not merely be sensitive to their environment but would receive from everything around them a sensation of pain. Above all, mental ailments would spread very rapidly; epidemics of insanity would occur during the following decade. This was the danger—epidemic insanity—that faced mankind, and the possibility of it in the future was why the leaders of humanity, the Masters of Wisdom, saw the necessity of allowing some spiritual wisdom to be diffused among mankind at large. Nothing short of a spiritual picture of the world could restore to coming generations a tendency to good health. Theosophy, you will realise, is thus a profound movement which has been given out to meet the needs of humanity. A hundred years ago a "nervous" man meant one with iron nerves. Simply from the change in the meaning of the word you can see that something quite new has come into the world.

How is the law of karma related to physical heredity? Physical heredity plays a great rôle; we know that some of the characteristics of a father and his ancestors may be found again in the son. In the Bach family, for instance, there were twenty-eight highly gifted musicians in a period of 250 years. Again, Bernoulli was a great mathematician, and eight other gifted mathematicians came after him in his family. This is all a matter of heredity, we are told; but that is only partially true. In order to be a good musician you need more than a musical predisposition in your soul; you need also a good ear in the physical sense. This good ear is a physical quality to be found in a family of musicians, and is passed on from one generation to the next. In a family, then, where a great deal of music is performed, you will find good musical ears, and so when a soul with a strongly developed musical talent is to be incarnated, it will naturally not choose a family with no interest in music—where it would languish—but one which has suitable physical organs. This fits in very well with the law of karma.

The same thing applies to moral courage. If a soul with that predisposition cannot find a suitable heredity, the characteristic will fade out. You can see that you have to be very careful in your choice of parents! The fact is not that the child resembles his parents, but that he is born into a family where the parents most resemble him.

You might ask: Does not this devalue a mother's love? Not at all. Just because the deepest sympathy already exists before birth, a particular child seeks out a particular mother; the love between them has its source much further back, and after birth it continues. The child loved its mother before it was born: no wonder then that the mother returns the love. Thus the significance of a mother's love is not falsely explained away; rather is its true source made clear. Of this, more tomorrow.

GOOD AND EVIL.
INDIVIDUAL KARMIC QUESTIONS

We will continue our study of particular karmic questions in relation to human life. What does occult science have to say about the origin of *conscience*? At our present stage of evolution conscience appears as a kind of inner voice telling us what to do and what to leave undone. How did such an inner voice come into being?

It is interesting to inquire whether in the historical evolution of mankind there has always been something comparable to what we call conscience. We find that in the earliest times, language had no word for it. In Greek literature it appears quite late, and in the language of the earlier Greeks no word for it exists. The same thing is true of the early periods of other civilisations. We may conclude, then, that the idea of conscience, in a more or less conscious form, came only gradually to be recognised. Conscience has developed fairly late in human evolution, and we shall see presently what our ancestors possessed in place of it.

How, then, has conscience gradually developed? On one of his journeys Darwin came across a cannibal and tried to convince him that it is not a good thing to eat another human being. The cannibal retorted that in order to decide whether eating a man is good or bad you must first eat one yourself. In other words, the cannibal had not reached the point of judging between good and bad in terms of moral ideas, but in accordance simply with the pleasure he experienced. He was in fact a survival from an earlier stage of civilisation which was at one time universal. But how does a man like this cannibal come to distinguish between good and bad? He went on eating his fellow-men until one day he was due to be eaten himself. At that moment he experienced the fact that it could really happen to him. He felt that there was something wrong about this, and the fruits of this experience remained with him in Kamaloka and Devachan. Into his next incarnation he brought a dim feeling that what he had been doing was not quite right. This feeling became more and more definite in the course of further incarnations; he also came to take heed of the feelings of others, and thus he gradually developed a certain restraint. After various further incarnations the feeling became still more definite and gradually the thought emerged: Here is something one should not do. Similarly, a savage at a primitive stage would eat everything indiscriminately, but when he got stomach-ache he came to realise by degrees that there were some things he could eat and some he could not. This kind of experience became gradually more and more firmly rooted, and finally it developed into the voice of conscience.

Conscience is therefore the outcome of experiences spread over a number of incarnations. Fundamentally, all knowledge, from the highest to the lowest, is the outcome of what a man has experienced; it has come into being as a result of trial and error.

An interesting fact is relevant here. Only since Aristotle has there been a science of logic, of logical thought. From this we must conclude that accurate thinking too, was born at a certain time. This is indeed so: thinking itself had first to evolve, and logical thinking arose in the course of time from fundamental observation of how thinking can go wrong. Knowledge is something mankind has acquired through many incarnations. Only after long trial and error could a store of knowledge be built up. All this illustrates the importance of the law of karma; here we have another example of something which has developed out of experience into a permanent habit and inclination. A motive such as conscience binds itself to the etheric body, becoming in time a permanent characteristic of it because the astral body has been so often convinced that this or that would not do.

Another interesting karmic relationship is between an

habitually selfish attitude and a loving sympathy with others. Some people are hardened egoists—not only in their acquisitiveness—and others are unselfish and sympathetic. Both attitudes depend on the etheric body and may even find expression in the physical body. People who in one life have been habitually selfish will age quickly in their next life; they seem to shrivel up. On the other hand, if in one life you have been ready to make sacrifices and have loved others you will remain young and hale. In this way you can prepare even the physical body for the next life.

If you recall what I said yesterday, you will have in mind a question: How is it with the achievements of the physical body itself? Its deeds become its future destiny; but what is the effect of any illnesses it may have had in this life?

The answer to this question, however strange it may sound, is not mere theory or speculation, but is based on occult experience, and from it you can learn the mission of illness. Fabre d'Olivet, who has investigated the origins of the Book of Genesis, once used a beautiful simile, comparing destiny with a natural process. The valuable pearl, he says, derives from an illness: it is a secretion of the oyster, so that in this case life has to fall sick in order to produce something precious. In the same way, physical illnesses in one life reappear in the next life as physical beauty. Either the physical body becomes more beautiful as a result of the illness endured; or it may be that an illness a man has caught from infection in his environment is compensated by the beauty of his new environment. Beauty thus develops, karmically, out of pain, suffering, privation and illness. This may seem a startling connection, but it is a fact. Even the appreciation of beauty develops in this way: there can be no beauty in the world without pain and suffering and illness. The same general law holds for the history of man's evolution. You will see from this how wonderful karmic relationships really are, and how questions about evil, illness and pain cannot be answered without knowledge of the important inner relationships within the evolution of humanity.

The line of evolution goes back into ancient, very ancient times, when conditions on Earth, and the Earth itself, were quite different. There was a time when none of the higher animals existed; when there were no fishes, amphibians, birds or mammals, but only animals less developed than the fishes. Yet man, though in a quite different form, was already there. His physical body was still very imperfect; his spiritual body was more highly developed. He was still enclosed within a soft etheric body, and his soul worked on his physical body from outside. Man still contained all other beings within himself. Later on he worked his way upwards and left behind the fish form which had been part of himself. These fish forms were huge, fantastic-looking creatures, unlike the fishes of today. Then again man evolved to a higher stage and cast out the birds from himself. Then the reptiles and amphibia made their way out of man—grotesque creatures such as the saurians and water-tortoises, which were really stragglers from an earlier group of beings, even further removed from man, whose evolution had lagged behind. Then man cast out the mammals from himself, and finally the apes; and then he himself continued to advance.

Man has therefore always been man and not an ape; he separated off the whole animal kingdom from himself so that he might become more truly human. It was as though you gradually strained all the dye-stuffs out of a coloured liquid and left only clear water behind. In older days there were natural philosophers, such as Paracelsus and Oken, who put this very well. When a man looks at the animal world, they said, he should tell himself: "I carried all that within myself and cast it out from my own being."

Thus man once had within himself a great deal that was later externalised. And today he still has within him something that later on will be outside—his karma, both the good and the evil. Just as he has separated the animals from himself, so will he thrust good and evil out into the world. The good will result in a race of men who are naturally good; the evil in a separate evil race. You will find this stated in the Apocalypse, but it must not be misunderstood. We must distinguish between the development of the soul and that of races. A soul may be incarnated in a race on the down grade, but if it does not itself commit evil, it need not incarnate a second time in such a race; it may incarnate in one that is ascending. There are quite enough souls streaming in from other directions to incarnate in these declining races.

But what is inward has to become outward, and man will rise still higher when his karma has worked itself out. With all this something of extraordinary interest is connected. Centuries ago, with the future development of humanity in view, secret Orders which set themselves the highest conceivable tasks were established. One such Order was the Manichean, of which ordinary scholarship gives a quite false picture. The Manicheans are supposed to have taught that a Good and an Evil are part of the natural order and have always been in conflict with one another, this having been determined for them by the Creation. Here there is a glimmer of the Order's real task, but distorted to the point of nonsense. The individual members of the Order were specially trained for their great work. The Order knew that some day there will be men in whose karma there is no longer any evil, but that there will also be a race evil by nature, among whom all kinds of evil will be developed to a higher degree than in the most savage animals, for they will practise evil consciously, exquisitely, with the aid of highly developed intellects. Even now the Manichean Order is training its members so that they may be able to transform evil in later generations.

The extreme difficulty of the task is that these evil races will not be like bad children in whom there is goodness which can be brought out by precept and example. The members of the Manichean Order are already learning how to transform quite radically those who by nature are wholly evil. And then the transformed evil will become a quite special good. The power to effect this change will bring about a condition of moral holiness on Earth. But this can be achieved only if the evil has first come into existence; then the power needed to overcome the evil will yield a power that can reach the heights of holiness. A field has to be treated with manure and the manure has to ferment in the soil; similarly, humanity needs the manure of evil in order to attain to the highest holiness. And herein lies the mission of evil. A man's muscles get strong by use; and equally, if good is to rise to the heights of holiness, it must first overcome the evil which opposes it. The task of evil is to promote the ascent of man. Things such as this give us a glimpse into the secret of life. Later on, when man has overcome evil, he can go on to redeem the creatures he has thrust down, and at whose cost he has ascended. That is the purpose of evolution.

The following point is rather more difficult. The shell of a snail or mussel is secreted out of the living substance of the animal. The shell which surrounds the snail was originally inside its body: its house is in fact its body in a more solid form. Theosophy tells us that we are one with all that surrounds us: this means that man at one time contained everything within himself. The Earth's crust, in fact, had its origin in man, who in the far past crystallised it out from within himself. Just as the snail at one time had its house within itself, so man had all other beings and kingdoms, minerals, plants and animals, within himself, and can say to them all: The substances were within me; I have crystallised out their constituent parts. Thus when man looks at anything outside himself, it becomes intelligible for him to say: All that is myself.

Even more subtle is a further idea. Imagine that ancient condition of humanity when nothing had yet been separated off from man. Man was there, and he formed mental pictures but they were not objective—not, that is, caused by external objects making an impression on him—they were purely subjective. Everything had its origin in man. Our dreams are still a legacy from the time when man, as it were, spun the whole world out of himself. Then he was able to look on the world over against himself. We as human beings have made everything, and in the rest of creation we can see our own products, our own being which has taken solid form.

Kant speaks of the thing-in-itself as something unknowable by man. But in fact there are no limits to knowledge, for man can find, in everything he sees around him, the traces of his own being, left behind.

All this has been said in order to show you that nothing can be truly understood if it is looked at from one side only. Everything which appears to us in one condition was quite different in earlier times; only by relating the present to the past can it be understood. Similarly, if you do not look beyond the physical world of the senses, you will never understand illness, or the mission of evil. In all such relationships there is a deep meaning. Evolution had to take its course in this way, through a process of splitting off, because man was to become an inward being; he had to put all this out of himself in order that he might be able to see his own self. So we can come to understand the mission of illness, of evil, and even of the external world. We are led to these great interconnections by studying the law of karma.

We will now deal with several particular questions about karma which are often asked. What is the karmic reason that causes many people to die young, even in childhood? From individual instances known to occult science we may come to the following conclusion. If we study a child who has died young, we may find that in his previous life he had good abilities and made good use of them. He was a thoroughly competent member of society, but he was rather short-sighted. Because with his weak eyes he could not see clearly, all his experiences acquired a particular colouring. He was wanting in a small matter which could have been better, and because of his weak eyes he always lagged behind. He could have achieved something quite remarkable if he had had good sight. He died, and after a short interval he was incarnated with healthy eyes, but he lived only a few weeks. By this means the members of his being learnt how to acquire good eyes, and he had gained a small portion of life as a corrective of what had been lacking in his previous life. The grief of his parents will, of course, be compensated for karmically, but in this instance they had to serve as instruments for putting the matter right.

What is the karmic explanation of children born dead? In such cases the astral body may well have already united itself with the physical body, and the two lower members may be properly constituted. But the astral body withdraws, and so the child is born dead. But why does the astral body withdraw? The explanation lies in the fact that certain members of man's higher nature are related to certain physical organs. For instance, no being can have an etheric body unless it possesses cells. A stone has no cells or vessels, and so it cannot have an etheric body. Equally, an astral body needs a nervous system: a plant has no nervous system and therefore cannot have an astral body. In fact, if a plant were to be permeated by an astral body it would no longer be a plant; it would have to be provided with a nervous system, just as the stone would have to be given cells if it were to have an etheric body.

Now if the Ego-body is gradually to find a place for itself, there must be warm blood in the physical body. (All red-blooded animals were separated off from man at the time when the Ego-condition was being prepared for man.) Hence it will be seen that the physical organs must be in proper condition if the higher bodies are to dwell within them. It is important to remember that the form of the physical body is moulded by purely physical inheritance. It may also happen that the way in which the various bodily fluids are combined is at fault, although parents are well-matched in soul and spirit. Then the incarnating entity comes to a physical body which cannot house the higher members of its being. Thus for example the physical and etheric bodies may be properly united; then the astral body ought to take possession of the physical body, but the

74

organism at its disposal is not in a suitable condition, and so it has to withdraw. The physical body remains, and is then still-born. A still-birth may thus be the outcome of a faulty mixture, on the physical level, of the fluids of the body, and this, too, will have a karmic connection. The physical body can thrive only in so far as the higher principles can live within it.

How are karmic compensations accomplished? If someone has done something to another person, there will have to be a karmic adjustment between them, which means that the persons concerned must be born again as contemporaries. How does this happen? What are the forces that bring the two persons together?

The way it works out is as follows. A wrong has been done; the victim has suffered it; the person who did it passes into Kamaloka, but first he has to witness the occurrence in the retrospective tableau of his past life. The injury he has inflicted does not then cause him pain, but in Kamaloka, as he relives his life backwards, the event comes before him, and now he has to suffer the pain he caused. He has to feel it in and through the very self of his victim. This experience imprints itself like a seal on his astral body. He takes with him a portion of the pain, and a definite force remains in him as the outcome of what he has experienced in the other man's being. In this way any pain or pleasure he has to live through turns into a force, and he carries a great number of such forces with him into Devachan.

When he returns to a new incarnation, this is the force that draws together all the persons who have had experiences in common. During the Kamaloka period they lived within one another, and they incorporated these forces into themselves. Hence within one physical human being there may be three or even more "Kamaloka men", in order that the situation involving them may be lived out.

An example known to occult science will make this clear. A man was condemned to death by five judges. What was really happening there? In a previous life the man had killed these other five men and karmic forces had brought all six together for a karmic adjustment. This does not produce a never-ending karmic chain; other relationships come in to change the further course of events.

Spiritual forces, you see, are thus secretly at work to bring about the complicated patterns of human living. Further important aspects of the subject will become clear during the next few days, when we go on to study the whole evolution of Earth and Man.

EVOLUTION OF THE EARTH

If we ask how man has developed since the earliest times up to the present day, we must first recall what has been said about the being of man. Man has seven members: the first is, so to speak, the lowest; the etheric body is higher and of finer texture; the astral body is still higher and finer; of the Ego-body only the first rudiments yet exist. It would be wrong to conclude that the highest body now possessed by man is the most perfect, and the physical body the most imperfect. Exactly the opposite is true: the physical body is the most perfect part of the human being. Later on the higher members will of course reach a higher degree of perfection, but at present the physical body is in its way the most highly developed and has been constructed with ineffable wisdom. I once described to you, as an example of this wisdom and perfection, the structure of the thigh-bone. Every single bone is so artistically structured and wisely devised as to perform the maximum work with the minimum mass, in a way no human engineer could equal.

The more deeply we penetrate to an understanding of the wonderful structure of the human frame, the more marvellous will it appear to us to be. Take, for instance, the way in which the brain and heart have been designed. The heart makes no mistakes, but the astral body makes many. The passions and desires of the astral body surge against the physical body and overpower it. If a man eats the wrong sort of food, he is following the desires of his astral body. The physical heart keeps the circulation of the blood in order; the astral body incessantly attacks the heart, because it craves for things harmful to the heart. Coffee, tea, alcohol, are poisons for the heart, yet the heart often has to cope with them every day, and in spite of everything it keeps going. It is constructed so durably that it can withstand the attacks of the astral body for seventy or eighty years. The physical body is thus in all details the most perfect in the hierarchy of human bodies.

Less perfect is the etheric body, and still less so the astral; the Ego-body is the least developed of them all. The reason is that the physical body has gone through the longest period of evolution and is the oldest part of the human being; younger is the etheric body, still younger the astral, and the Ego-body is the youngest of all.

In order to understand how these bodies have evolved, we must realise that it is not only man who goes through successive incarnations, but that the law of reincarnation applies universally. All beings, and all the planets, are subject to this law. The Earth, with everything that is on it, has passed through earlier incarnations, of which three in particular are our immediate concern.

Before the Earth became the planet we know, it was a very different one. At the beginning of time it was a planet called, in occult science, Saturn. Altogether there have been four successive incarnations of the Earth: Saturn, Sun, Moon and Earth. Just as there is a Kamaloka and Devachan period between a man's successive incarnations, so is there between successive incarnations of a planet, a period when it is not visible and has no outward life. This period has always been called Pralaya, and the period of incorporation, Manvantara. However, the names Saturn, Sun and Moon do not signify the heavenly bodies which are called so today. Our Sun is a fixed star; the old Sun was a planet, and in the course of its incarnations it has worked itself up from the substance and being of a planet to the rank of a fixed star. In the same way the Old Moon, as we call it, is not the same as the Moon we know today; it was the third incarnation of the Earth. Similarly with Saturn, the first stage of the Earth's evolution.

Even on the planet Saturn man was present. Saturn did not shine, but it sounded and could have been heard with

Devachanic ears. After existing for a certain period it gradually vanished away, was for a long time invisible, and then shone out as Sun. The planet Sun passed through the same process and reappeared as Moon. Finally, after the same sequence, the Earth appeared.

But we must not picture these four planets—Saturn, Sun, Moon and Earth—as four separate planets; they are four different conditions of the same planet. They are true metamorphoses of the one planet and all the beings that belong to it are metamorphosed with it. Man has never been on any other planet, but the Earth has existed in these four different conditions.

When the Earth existed as Saturn, only the first germs of the kingdom of man dwelt on it. The marvellously artistic structure of the human body was then present only in barest outline. There were no minerals, plants or animals. Man is the first-born of our creative process. But Saturn-man was very different from the man of today. He was for the most part a spiritual being; he would not have been visible to physical eyes—and of course at that time there were none. Only a being with Devachanic sight could have perceived him. The human form was like a kind of auric egg, and within it was a remarkable scaly structure, a sort of vortex, shaped like a small pear and as though made of oyster-shells. Saturn was permeated with these rudimentary physical structures—exudations, as it were, condensed out of the spiritual. From these structures, which gave only a faint indication of what they were to become, the physical body of man was gradually developed in the course of evolution. It was a kind of primal mineral, with no etheric body round it; hence we can say that man passed through the mineral kingdom; but to think of it as anything like our present-day mineral kingdom would be quite wrong. On Saturn there was no kingdom other than the human kingdom.

Now just as man passes through the various stages of his life, as child, young man or woman, old man or woman, so does a planet. Before Saturn manifested the flaky structures deposited within it, it was an Arupa-Devachan structure, then a Rupa-Devachan structure, and finally an astral structure. Then the flakes gradually disappear, and Saturn returns through the same stages into the darkness of Pralaya. A metamorphosis such as this, from the spiritual into the physical and then back again into the spiritual, is called in Theosophy a Round, or a Life-condition. Each Round can be divided into seven phases: Arupa, Rupa, Astral, Physical and back to Arupa. These phases, called "Globes", are Form-conditions. But we must not imagine seven successive Globes; it is always the same planet which transforms itself, and its beings are transformed with it. Saturn passes through seven such Rounds or Life-conditions. In each Round its structure was being perfected, so that only in the seventh Round was its finally perfected form attained. Each Round has its seven transformations, or Form-conditions, so that Saturn will have passed through seven times seven, or forty-nine, metamorphoses. That is true of Saturn, and then of Sun, Moon and Earth; and in the future there will be three more planets: Jupiter, Venus and Vulcan.

There are thus seven planets, each going through seven Rounds and each Round through seven Form-conditions, expressed as 777 in occult script. In that script, 7 in the unit position means the Globes; in the tens, the Rounds, and in the hundreds, Planets. We therefore have to multiply the figures, and so we find that our planetary system has to pass through 7 by 7 by 7, or 343 transformations.

In H. P. Blavatsky's *Secret Doctrine*, which was in large part inspired by one of the highest spiritual individualities, we find a remarkable passage. But the great Initiates have always expressed themselves with caution and have given only hints; above all they leave some work for the human being to do. This passage, as H.P.B. knew very well, is full of riddles. There is nothing there about successive incarnations; the teacher said only, "Learn the riddle of 777". His wish was that people should learn for themselves that this meant 343. *The Secret Doctrine* gives the riddle but not the solution: this has been discovered only quite recently.

The first germinal condition of man was thus to be found on Saturn in the most ancient times. Then Saturn vanished into Pralaya, and reappeared as Sun, and with it from the darkness of Pralaya came man, the ancient inhabitant of the Universe. In the meantime, however, man had gained the power to separate something from out of himself as the snail does its shell. He could separate shell-like structures as hovering forms; the finer substances he retained within himself so that he might evolve to a higher level. In this way he formed the minerals from out of himself, but these minerals were a kind of living minerals. On Sun, man evolved in such a way that the etheric body, as with planets today, could be added. Thus on Sun he passed through the plant stage, and on Sun there were thus two kingdoms, the mineral kingdom and the plant kingdom; and the latter was man. But these plant forms were quite different from those we know today.

Anyone who understands the deeper relationships will regard the plant as an inverted man. Below is its root; then come the stalk, leaves, stamens and pistils; the pistils contain the female reproductive organs and the stamens, the male. In all innocence the plant stretches out its reproductive organs to the Sun, for it is the Sun that kindles its reproductive power. The root is really the "head" of the plant, which stretches its reproductive organs out to the wide spaces of the world, while its head is attracted by the centre of the Earth. Man is the opposite of this: his head is at the top of his body, and below are the organs which the plant spreads out to the Sun. The animal comes in between: its body is horizontal. If you revolve a plant through 90 degrees, you get the position of the animal; turn it through 180 degrees and you get the position of man.

The old occult science gave expression to this in the ancient symbol of the Cross, saying, as Plato said in the language of the old Mysteries: the World-Soul is crucified on the cross of the World-Body. The World-Soul is contained in everything, but it has to work its way up through these three stages; it makes its journey on the cross of the body of the world.

On Sun, then, man was a plant-being, upside down compared with modern man. He lived in the Sun and was himself part of its body. The Sun was a body of light, composed of light-ether; man was still plant-like, his head directed towards the centre of the Sun. When later on the Sun left the Earth, the human plant had to turn round; it remained true to the Sun.

In its first Round, Sun merely repeated the Saturn period: it was not until the second Round that the further evolution of man began. When the Sun had evolved to its limit in the seven Rounds, it disappeared into the darkness of Pralaya, and eventually reappeared as Moon.

The first Moon-Round was again only a repetition of Saturn in a rather different form. The second Round also brought nothing new; it was a recapitulation of life on the Sun. In the third Round there was something new: man acquired an astral body in addition to the two earlier bodies. In his outward form we might compare him to the animals of today, for he had three bodies. He had in fact reached the stage of the animal kingdom. He had raised himself to the plant kingdom by ejecting the mineral kingdom. Thus there were two kingdoms apart from man. Then he once more cast off a smaller part, separated himself from it, and went on to the higher level.

During this third Round of Moon an important cosmic event took place. Sun and Moon separated, so there were now two bodies. At the beginning of the second Round the Sun was still there unchanged; then a small segment in the lower part of the Sun detached itself, so that in the third Round there were two bodies side by side.

The Sun kept the finer parts, sending rays to the Moon from the outside, and providing the Moon and all the beings with what they needed. This was the advancement of the Sun; it became a fixed star, and is no longer concerned directly with the three kingdoms; it only imparts to them what it has to give. It gave a home to higher Beings who, now that the Sun had got rid of its inferior parts, could develop further. In the fourth Round all this reached its highest possible level; in the fifth the two bodies reunited and finally disappeared as one body into Pralaya.

The Old Moon had as yet no solid mineral kingdom. It was a globe which, instead of a solid earth crust, had something like a living and inwardly growing peaty mass. This living foundation was permeated with woody structures out of which grew the plant kingdom, as it then was. These plants, however, were really a sort of "plant-animal": they were able to feel and under pressure would have experienced pain. And man in the animal kingdom of the time was not like any animal of today; he was halfway between animal and man. He was of a higher order than our present animals and could carry out his impulses in a much more systematic way. But he was lower than modern man, for he was not able to say "I" to himself. He did not yet possess an Ego-body.

These three kingdoms dwelt on the living body of the Moon. An important fact is that these Moon-men did not breathe as man does today; they breathed fire, not air. Through this breathing in of fire the warmth permeated their whole being; then they breathed out the fire and heat became cold again. What man has nowadays as the heat of his blood, Moon-men had in the warmth of their breath. Many of the older, still clairvoyant painters symbolised this in the image of the fire-breathing dragon; they knew that in ancient times there had been these Moon-beings who breathed fire.

After disappearing into Pralaya, the Moon reappeared as Earth. In the first Round the whole Saturn-existence was repeated, in the second the Sun, and in the third the Moon-existence. During the third Round the separation of Sun and Moon was repeated, but on the returning path of this Round two bodies reunited.

83

In the fourth Round the Sun and Moon came forth again as one body, and now the Earth began to form itself. At this point an important event occurred: an encounter of the Earth with the planet Mars. The planets interpenetrated, the Earth going through Mars. At that time Mars possessed a substance, iron, which the Earth lacked, and Mars left this iron in the Earth in a vaporous form. But for this occurrence, the Earth would have had to remain as it was, possessing only what was already there. Man would have risen as far as the animal kingdom, as it then was; he would have breathed warmth, but he would never have acquired warm blood, for there is iron in the blood. In fact, according to occult science the Earth is indebted to Mars to such an extent that the first half of its evolution is called Mars. Mercury has equal significance for the second half; the Earth entered into a connection with Mercury and is still closely related to it. Hence in occult science the terms *Mars* and *Mercury* are used instead of *Earth.*

This planetary stage will be followed in the future by three others: Jupiter, Venus, Vulcan. These seven stages of the Earth, as recorded in occult science, are preserved in the days of the week, though in German they are somewhat confused:

Saturn	Saturday, Samedi	Samstag
Sun	Sunday	Sonntag
Moon	Monday, Lundi	Montag
Mars	Mardi, or Tiu—Tuesday	Dienstag
Mercury	Mercredi, Wednesday	Mittwoch
Jupiter	Jeudi, Tor, Donar—Thursday	Donnerstag
Venus	Vendredi, Freya—Friday	Freitag

Thus do the names of the days of the week reflect the occult doctrine of the passage of the Earth through these various stages: a remarkable chronicle which makes it possible for these truths to be kept ever and again in mind.

We shall see in the course of the next few days how Theosophy enables us to understand for the first time what our early forefathers expressed quite simply in names, and how the most ordinary everyday things are linked with the most profound.

PROGRESS OF MANKIND UP TO ATLANTEAN TIMES

When the Earth reappeared out of the darkness of Pralaya, it did not emerge alone; it was at first united with the Sun and our present Moon. Sun, Moon and Earth formed one huge body. This was the first stage of our planet.

At that time the Earth consisted of a very, very tenuous substance. There were no solid minerals, no water, only this subtle material we call ether. The whole body was thus a planet made up of fine etheric material and surrounded by an atmosphere of spirit, in the same way as our own Earth is surrounded by air. This spirit-atmosphere contained everything which today constitutes the human soul. Your souls, which today have come down into your bodies, were at that time up above in this spirit-atmosphere. The Earth was a vast globe of ether, very much bigger than our Earth today, and surrounded by spiritual substance which contained the souls of mankind. Down below, in the rarefied substance of the etheric globe, something rather denser was present— millions of shell-like forms. These were the human germs of the Saturn stage, now emerging as a recapitulation of the forms developed on Saturn in ancient times.

There was of course no possibility of physical reproduction or increase; a quite different process prevailed in those times. The whole of the spirit-atmosphere was, like our present atmosphere, a more or less homogeneous whole, except that spiritual offshoots rather like tentacles stretched down from it into the etheric globe and enveloped the shell-like forms. You must picture the spirit descending from above and enfolding each individual body. A tentacle worked on a body and built up a human form. When one form was complete, the tentacle withdrew, stretched itself in another direction and went to work on another body. The resulting forms were thus brought forth directly by the spiritual worlds. In the beginning there was a confused interwoven ether-substance, much denser than the homogeneous divine-spiritual substance which stretched forth its arms to create the forms out of chaos. This first epoch of our Earth is well described in the book of Genesis: "In the beginning God created Heaven and Earth and the Earth was without form, and void, and the spirit of God moved on the face of the waters." The ether, as it then was, is called "water" in occult science.

You could not then have seen the Earth or the shell-like forms; they were resounding human forms, and each one, as it came into being, expressed itself through a specific note. The forms possessed no individuality, for individuality was still dissolved in the spirit-atmosphere. Seven kinds of forms could be distinguished by their ground-notes. These seven groups constituted the first human Root-race.

After millions of years a great cosmic event took place: the whole vast ether-body contracted and assumed a biscuit-like shape which it retained for a period. Finally a small part, consisting of Earth and Moon, separated off from the whole. An important stage in human evolution is bound up with this occurrence. The germinal human forms were differentiated and articulated; and because of the departure of the Sun, objects could now for the first time be illuminated from outside. All our seeing depends on the fact that the Sun's rays fall on some object and are reflected back. When the Sun withdrew, there were now bodies in existence on which it could shine, and this led to the development of an organ of sight, for light is truly the creator of the eyes. The germinal human forms, which had hitherto been maintained by the common divine atmosphere, could now see their environment. This period is described in Genesis with the words: "And God said, Let there be light: and there was light. And God saw the light that it was good: and God divided the light from the darkness." The whole of the

Earth's body now began to revolve and thus there were day and night. When we read the Bible in the light of occult science, we can again take it all literally.

A great number of the spiritual Beings who had surrounded the Earth had gone forth with the Sun. They formed the spiritual population of the Sun and exerted their influence on the Earth from the Sun. The etheric human forms were now furnished with an astral covering. The united body of Earth and Moon was surrounded by an astral atmosphere which had previously been dissolved in the spiritual atmosphere. The ether, which had earlier existed as the basic substance, had now condensed into independent etheric bodies surrounding the separate physical forms, which in their turn had become denser.

In contrast to the etheric body, however, the astral body had as yet no independent existence: there was still a common astral covering for all beings. This was the Earth-spirit, which now again stretched forth its tentacles and enveloped each single human ancestor. And now a new faculty appeared: each human form could produce another out of its own substance—a sort of reproduction without fertilisation between two beings. When the fertilisation withdrew from one form, it sank into another without a break. It was rather the same as when part of the front of a cloud detaches itself and is immediately replaced by another part from behind. It was no more than a metamorphosis; as uninterrupted continuity of consciousness prevailed. The experience was like that of a simple change of clothes. The whole planet was bathed in wonderful beauty; it floated in glorious colours in the light-ether, and gradually condensed.

Side by side with the ancestors of humanity there were already forms of plants and animals, destined to be man's companions. The plants were of the lower types which have now become dwarfed. The animals, too, had not yet acquired their present-day shapes. There were shining plants and animals that whirled through the ether. All were still of one sex, except that certain animals were beginning to develop bi-sexual rudiments. There was still no real mineral kingdom. Then the etheric forms gradually became more and more densified, with increasing absorption of the astral element.

After the passing of a further million years or so, Earth and Moon had acquired a very different appearance. Animals and plants were now like jelly or white of egg, rather like some of our jelly-fishes and sea-plants. In this more condensed form of matter were to be found the ancestors of humanity, with rudimentary organs. The forms of animals and plants were increasingly densified by the fertilising astral force. Then came an important stage when the fertilising Beings in the astral atmosphere permeated the nature-forms of that time, so that man and animals were able to draw directly from the vegetable kingdom the substances they needed for nourishment and for reproduction. The plants secreted a substance rather like present-day milk; a last survivor of these milk-secreting plants is the dandelion. So the human beings of that time were nourished and fertilised by the nature around them, and they were self-less. They were complete vegetarians, absorbing only what nature freely offered, and living on juices similar to milk and honey. It was a wonderful state of existence in those primeval days, scarcely describable in our modern language.

Then came an immensely important event: Earth and Moon separated. The smaller body of the Moon split off from the Earth. Now there were three bodies: Sun, Moon and Earth. This had far-reaching consequences for all living beings: the Moon carried off with it a great part of the forces that human beings and animals needed in order to reproduce themselves. Each individual now had only half the fertilising power he had previously possessed, and the result was a gradual emergence of two sexes. Man now had to receive the fertilising power from another being like himself. This was the Lemurian epoch, that of the third Root-race.

During this period, too, matter began to become harder and more solid. Shortly before the separation of Earth and

Moon denser deposits had been formed, and after the separation cartilaginous substances, leading towards bone-formation, began to appear in the bodies of men and animals. The solidity of the bones developed, in correspondence with the solidifying of the Earth's crust. By degrees, solid mineral forms appeared. Previously, everything had been etheric, then airy, then watery; the various beings swam as though in water or flew as though in air. Now the Earth developed a solid skeleton of rocks, parallel with the development of the human skeletons. Bone-formation and rock-formation went hand in hand. The human form at that time was something like a fish-bird-animal. Most of the Earth was still watery and the temperature was still very high. This watery element contained in solution much that later on became solid—our present-day metals, for instance, and other substances. Human beings moved in it with a swimming, floating motion. They were well able to endure the tremendous heat which reigned on Earth; their bodies were still constituted of a material which corresponded to the prevailing conditions, and in this way they could live.

Small continents on which men could roam about were embedded like islands in the water; but the whole Earth was riddled with volcanic activity which constantly destroyed parts of the Earth with immense violence, so that elemental destruction and rebuilding went on continually, turn by turn.

As yet man had no lungs; he breathed through tubular gills. But he was already a very complex organism; he had deposited in himself a backbone, at first cartilaginous and then bony, and in order to propel himself as he floated and swam he had a swim-bladder, rather like that of some present-day fish.

Soon—but this means after millions of years—the Earth became more solid. The water withdrew and separated from the solid parts; the air developed its own purity, and under the influence of the air the swim-bladder changed into lungs. Man now raised himself out of the watery element—a specially important and significant event. The gills were transformed into organs of hearing. With the development of lungs, man learnt to breathe, and then all mankind lived in a common element, the air. Each human being breathed in his portion of air, shaped it to his own fire, and breathed it out again. In the beginning, therefore, man was filled with pure spirit, later with the astral element, and finally with air. As soon as he had reached the stage where the breathing of heat was transformed into the breathing of air, that which Mars had provided was turned to good account; human blood became warm. The moment had come when something spiritual which had previously surrounded man entered into him—and how? Through the air. The capacity to breathe signifies the acquisition of the individual human spirit. The Ego enters into him together with the air he breathes. If we speak of an Ego common to all men, it also has a common body, the air. Not without reason did the ancients call this universal Ego, Atma—*Atmen,* the breath. They knew very well that they drew it in with the breath and breathed it out again. We live in one common Ego because we live in the all-pervading air. Of course the event I have been describing must not be taken too literally. The sinking down of the individual Ego into man is spoken of in theosophical literature as the descent of Manas, or Manasaputra. With every breath, man slowly took in Manas, Buddhi and Atma, more or less germinally. Genesis describes this moment and we can take it literally: "And God breathed into Adam the breath of life, and Adam was a living soul." This is the reception of the individual spirit.

Man now had warm blood also, and was thus able to retain warmth permanently within himself. And with this something further of great importance is bound up.

On the Old Moon there were Beings who were at a higher stage of evolution than the humanity of that time: these were the gods who in Christian tradition are called Angels and Archangels. They had once been at the human stage, but in the course of time they had ascended higher, just as we, too, will have ascended higher when we reach the next planetary stage. Although they no longer had a physical body, they were still connected with the Earth. They were no longer subject to human needs, but they needed men to rule over.

When the Old Moon had completed its evolution, some of these gods had not fully evolved with it; they had to remain as they were. They had not progressed as far as they should have done. Thus there were beings halfway between gods and men—demi-gods. They became quite especially important for the Earth and for humanity. They could not rise completely beyond the human sphere, but equally they could not incarnate in human bodies. They could establish themselves only in one part of human nature, so as to use this part for furthering their own evolution and at the same time to help mankind. On the Moon they had breathed fire, and in the fire which had become permanent in man, in the warm human blood—the original seat of passions and desires —they took up their abode, and imparted to man some of the fire which had been their element on the Moon. These are the hosts of Lucifer, the Luciferic beings: the Bible calls them the tempters of humanity. They tempted man in so far as they lived in his blood and gave him independence. Without these Luciferic beings, everything would have come to man as a gift from the gods. Man would have been wise, but not independent; enlightened, but not free. Because these beings anchored themselves in his blood, man not only became wise, but could be fired with enthusiasm for wisdom and ideals.

At the same time, however, the possibility of error arose: man was now able to turn his back on the highest and to choose between good and evil. The Lemurian race gradually evolved with this disposition, this inherent possibility of evil, and in consequence the Earth had to endure great upheavals, convulsions and earthquakes. In the end, Lemuria was destroyed through these passionate impulses of mankind.

Meanwhile, the Earth had undergone further changes and

had become more solid. Other continents had arisen, and most important among them was Atlantis, between present-day Europe, Africa and America. The descendants of the Lemurian race had spread over this continent. In the course of millions of years they had greatly changed, and had acquired a form which resembled the form of man today. Yet they were very different from modern man. The shape of the head and forehead was quite different; the forehead was much lower and the digestive organs were much more powerful. The etheric body of an Atlantean extended far beyond and around his head. In the etheric body there was an important point which corresponded with a point in the physical head. In the course of Atlantean evolution the two points drew together, until the point in the etheric body sank into the physical. At the moment when these two points coincided, man could begin to say "I" to himself. The forepart of the brain could now develop as an instrument for the spirit; self-consciousness began. All this happened first among those Atlanteans who dwelt in the neighbourhood of modern Ireland.

The Atlanteans gradually evolved through seven sub-races: Rmoahals, Tlavatli, and primal Toltecs, Turanians, Semites, Akkadians and Mongols. It was among the primal Semites that the unification of the two points first occurred, and clear self-consciousness arose. The two following sub-races, the primal Akkadians and Mongols, really overshot the goal of Atlantean humanity.

Until the two points were thus united, the soul-powers of the Atlanteans were fundamentally different from our own. The Atlanteans had a much more mobile body, and, especially in their early times, a very powerful will. They were able, for instance, to replace a lost limb; they could make plants grow, and so on. Thus they exercised a powerful influence over nature. Their sense-organs were more strongly developed: they could distinguish different metals by touch, just as we can distinguish smells. They still possessed also a high degree of clairvoyance. Their sleep at night was not like that of modern man, who mostly has only confused dreams; it was rather a dimmer sort of clairvoyance. During the night they were in touch with the gods, and what they experienced lived on in myths and legends. They pressed the powers of nature into their service; their dwellings were partly natural stuctures and partly hewn out of rocks. They constructed airships which were not propelled by inorganic forces, such as coal, but by the use of the organic, germinating power of plants.

As long as the two points I have mentioned were not yet united, the Atlanteans had no combinative intellect; for instance they could not count. But to make up for that they had particularly well-developed memories. A logical combinative intellect and self-consciousness emerged only with the fifth sub-race, the primal Semites.

Atlantis perished in a vast water-catastrophe; the whole continent was gradually flooded, and most of the people migrated eastward towards Europe and Asia. One of the main groups passed through Ireland and Europe to Asia; everywhere numbers of people remained behind. The Leader was a high Initiate in whom the migrants had complete faith; through his wisdom he picked out the best of them to accompany him to a distant part of Asia, where he settled them in the district now known as the Gobi Desert. There a small colony developed in complete isolation. From there colonisers went out into all inhabited lands and founded the civilisations of the next Root-race: the Indian, the Persian, the Egypto-Chaldean-Assyrian, the Graeco-Latin. And then the Anglo-Saxon-Germanic civilisation arose.

We shall see tomorrow how this development went on.

THE POST-ATLANTEAN CULTURE-EPOCHS

Yesterday I told you how the great Initiate selected from the primal Semites who were living in the neighbourhood of Ireland, a group of people whom he led towards the East and settled there. There Manu trained the chosen men to be the progenitors of the new civilisations. He taught them and gave them directions for a moral way of life, with everything laid down in the minutest detail. He taught them how to distribute their time and how to arrange their work from morning till evening. But even more than by his precepts he educated them by direct influence and by his thoughts. When he sent out his thoughts into the colony, his ideas and precepts acted by direct suggestion. This was the sort of influence needed by the men of that time for their training and re-moulding.

The following episode brings out the difference between the whole outlook of the Atlantean race and that of the new Root-race; it occurred in the middle of the nineteenth century. European colonists had induced some Red Indians —in whom we have to see the descendants of Atlanteans who had failed to make headway and had then become retrograde—to relinquish their lands on condition that new hunting-grounds were allotted to them. But the promise had not been kept and the Indian Chief could not understand this. Hence he addressed the Europeans as follows: "You Pale-faces promised us that your Chief would give our brothers other lands in place of those you have taken from us. Your feet are now on our land and you are walking over the graves of our brothers. The White Man has not kept the promise he made to the Brown Man. You Pale-faces have your black instruments with all kinds of little magic signs" —he meant their books—"from which you learn the will of your God. Your's must be a bad God if he does not teach his people to keep their word. The Brown-man's God is not like that; the Brown-man hears the thunder and sees the lightning and this language he can understand; his God speaks to him in this language. He hears the rustling of the leaves and trees in the woods, and in them also his God speaks to him. He hears the water rippling in the brook, and the Brown-man can understand that speech also. He knows when a storm is brewing. Everywhere he can hear his God speaking, and the lesson his God teaches is very different from what your magical black signs say to you."

This is really a very significant speech, for it contains a sort of confession of faith. The Atlantean did not raise himself to his God through concepts and ideas. He discerned something holy in nature as a keynote of the Divine; it was as though he breathed in and breathed out his God. If he wished to express what he heard in this way, he would embody it in a sound similar to the Chinese T-A-O. For the Atlantean this was the sound which pervaded the whole of nature. When he touched a leaf, or saw a flash of lightning, he was aware that part of the Godhead was displayed before him; it was as if he were touching the garment of the Divine. Just as we make contact with some element in a man's soul when we shake hands with him, so the Atlantean, when he took hold of a form in nature, felt that he was touching the body of the Godhead. He lived in a religious feeling quite different from our own. The Atlantean, too, was still clairvoyant and was thus in direct communication with the world of spirits.

But then the type of thinking associated with logic and mathematical calculation began to develop, and the more it did so, the more did clairvoyance fade away. People began to concern themselves more with what the senses could perceive externally, and so nature was increasingly divested of divinity. People acquired a new gift at the cost of an old one. In proportion as they achieved the gift of exact sense-observation, they ceased to understand nature as the body of the Godhead. Gradually they came to see before them only the body of the world, and not its soul. But as the result of this a yearning for the Divine arose once more in man. In his heart it was written: Behind nature there must be God. And he came to realise that he must seek for God with his spirit. That is in fact the meaning of the word 'religion': to try to re-establish a connection with the Godhead; *religere* means to re-unite.

Now there are various ways of finding the Godhead. The Indians, who were the first sub-race of the Aryan race, took the following way. Certain God-inspired messengers of Manu, called the holy Rishis, became the teachers of the ancient Indian culture. No poetry or tradition tells us about this— it is known only through what has been handed down orally in the occult schools. Poems such as the Vedas and the Bhagavad Gita, wonderful as they are, are of much later origin. The ancient Indian felt in his heart that external nature as he saw it was unreal, and that behind it the Godhead was concealed. The name he gave to this Godhead was Brahman, the hidden God. The whole external world was thus for him an illusion, deception, Maya. Whereas the Atlantean could still discern the Godhead in every leaf, the Indian said: "The Godhead is no longer apparent in the outer world. I must sink into my inner being and seek for Him in my heart; I must follow after Him towards a higher spiritual condition." In every approach to the Godhead there was still a dreamlike element. The Indian could find no Divinity in nature; it was in great and powerful thought-pictures, in visions and imaginations that the world of Brahman revealed itself to him. Yoga was the name of the training he had to undergo in order to penetrate through illusion to the spirit and the primal source of being. The profound Vedas, the Bhagavad Gita, that sublime song of human perfection, are only echoes of that ancient divine wisdom.

This was the first stage along the path by which humanity sought to return to the Godhead; it is a stage which could not achieve much in terms of external civilisation. The Indian turned away from everything external and looked for the higher life only in world-renouncing ascent to the Spirit.

The second sub-race, that of the ancient Persians, had a very different mission, although its culture originated from the clear purpose of Manu. Long before the time of Zarathustra, Persia had an ancient culture, of which only an oral tradition survives. People were now coming to the thought that external reality was an image of the Divine, which must not be turned away from but shaped anew. The Persian wished to transform nature by work; he became a husbandman. He moved out of the quiet realm of world-renouncing thoughts and learnt from the resistance he encountered that the outer world was not wholly Maya. Side by side with the world of Spirit he found a real world in which work had to be done. The conviction gradually grew within him that there are two worlds: the world of the good Spirit in which a man can immerse himself and the world which has to be worked upon. And then he said: In the world of the Spirit I shall find the ideas and concepts through which I may transform the world of external reality, so that it may itself become an image of the external Spirit.

Thus the Persian saw himself placed in a struggle between two worlds; and presently this took more and more the form of a conflict between two powers—Ormuzd, representing the world of the good Spirit, and Ahriman, representing the world which has to be transformed. But he found himself still at a loss in one respect: the outer world confronted him as something he could not understand; he could not discover any laws in it. He failed to see that the spiritual can be found in nature; he was aware only of nature's resistance to his work.

The third sub-race, comprising the Chaldean-Assyrian-Babylonian-Egyptian people, and later the Semites who branched off from them, came to understand these laws. Men looked up to the stars and observed their movements and their influence on human life, and accordingly worked out a science which enabled them to understand these movements and influences. They brought. the Heavens into connection with the Earth. We can see the character of this third sub-race from a particular example. The Egyptians observed that the flooding of the Nile, when it inundates the surrounding country, occurred at the time of the rising of a particular constellation, that of Sirius; and they connected the rising of the Nile with this constellation. Again, they observed the position of the Sun at the time of the arrival and departure of certain birds; they observed the rising and the setting of the stars, their relation to one another and to mankind, and so they gradually built up a science. It became clear to them that there was a great wisdom governing all natural processes; that everything happened in accordance with great laws, and these they tried to fathom. The ancient Chaldean priests, above all, were the custodians of profound wisdom, but for them these laws of nature were not merely abstract, nor were the stars merely physical globes. They looked on each planet as ensouled by a Being whose body it was. They had a quite concrete conception that behind every constellation was a divine Being which gave it life. Thus the Egyptians and Chaldeans discerned that they were spirits living among spirits in a world of spirits. They saw matter as filled with wisdom.

So humanity had gradually come by the path of knowledge to recognise the wisdom in external nature, and thus to rediscover something which the ancient Atlanteans had known through natural clairvoyance.

The fourth sub-race, the bearer of Graeco-Roman culture, was no longer directly influenced by Manu, but came under the influence of other cultures. It had a different mission— art. Little by little man had found the way to carry the spirit into nature. The Greek went further than the Egyptian: instead of taking the finished forms of nature, he took the still unformed substance of marble and impressed on it his own stamp. He formed his own gods, Zeus and the rest. The third sub-race had sought the spirit in the external world; the fourth impressed the spirit itself on the world. Art, the charming of spirit into matter, was the task reserved for the Graeco-Roman race.

The Egyptian studied the stars in their courses and in accordance with them he regulated his political institutions for centuries ahead. The Greek drew his ideas about the form of human society from his own inner life. The Roman went even further: he moulded the whole social life of human beings in accordance with his mind.

The Germans and Anglo-Saxons—the fifth sub-race, to which we ourselves belong—go very much further in moulding the external world. They not only imprint on matter something from within themselves; they discover divinely-ordained laws of nature and use them to alter the world. They discover the laws of gravity, of heat, of steam and electricity, and with their aid they transform the whole visible world. The mission of this fifth sub-race is to study not only the laws which slumber within mankind, but those which permeate the whole world, and then to imprint them on the external world. The result is that humanity has become more material, indeed materialistic. In this age no Zeus could arise, but—the steam engine!

We shall be succeeded by another race which will retrace the path to the spirit. The achievement of our race represents the highest point of man's power to transform the physical world. We have descended furthest into the physical plane and gone to the utmost limits in our conquest of it. This has been the mission of post-Atlantean humanity. The Indian turned away from the physical. The Persian saw it as a substance which resisted his efforts. The Chaldeans, Babylonians and Egyptians recognised the wisdom in nature. The Greeks and Romans went further in their conquest of the physical plane from within. Only our own culture has gone so far as to operate with the laws of nature on the physical plane. From now onwards mankind will become more spiritual again.

There is a great and powerful purpose in the course of

human evolution. Each group of peoples has its own task. Present-day man knows nothing of what the third and fourth sub-races still had in their myths and legends as re-collections of primal times and the world of the gods; he has only the physical plane. And through his descent to the physical plane he has lost his connection with the world of the gods. For him, only the physical world exists.

Theosophists are not reactionaries; they know that the age of materialism was necessary. Just as the organs of sight degenerate in animals when they go to live in dark caves, while other faculties develop more powerfully, so do we find the same thing happening in the world of the spirit and the world of the senses; if one faculty develops, another must fade away. The gift of clairvoyance and the power of memory had to withdraw in order that the power of physical sight could develop. When men learnt how to conquer the world by means of the laws of nature they had discover-ed, they had to sacrifice the power of seership.

How different earlier outlooks were! Copernicus, for instance, freed men from the mistaken idea that the Earth stands still. It was an error, he taught, to believe that the Sun moved round the Earth. His doctrine was further devel-oped by Kepler and Galileo. Yet Copernicus and Ptolemy were both right. It all depends on the stand-point from which you are looking at Sun and Earth. If you study our solar system from the astral and not from the physical plane, Ptolemy's system is right—there is the Earth at the centre and the situation is as the ancients described it. We need only remind ourselves that on the astral plane everything appears reversed. The Ptolemaic system holds good for the astral plane, the Copernican for the physical. In future times yet another, quite different picture of the world will prevail. Generally we hear that Copernicus taught only two things: that the Earth revolves on its own axis and that the Earth moves round the Sun. It is seldom noticed that he taught also a third form of movement—that the whole solar system moves onward in a spiral. For the present this fact will be left aside, but in the future humanity will return to it. Copernicus stood on a frontier, and the old outlook was strongly present in him.

There is no absolute truth—each truth has its particular mission at a certain time. We talk of Theosophy today, but we know that when we come to be reborn in the future, we shall hear something very different and stand in a quite different relationship to one another.

Let us cast our gaze back to a time when we were perhaps even then assembled together in some region of Northern Europe, where people gathered round a Druid priest who imparted truth to them in the form of myths and legends. If we had not heeded what he then said and if he had not influenced our souls, we should not be able today to understand the truth which Theosophy now brings to us in a different form. When we are reborn, we shall hear the truth spoken in another and a higher form. Truth evolves, as does everything else in the world. It is the form of the divine Spirit, but the divine Spirit has many forms. If we thoroughly imbue ourselves with this characteristic of truth, we shall acquire a quite different relation to it. We shall say: Indeed we live in the truth, but it can take many forms. And we shall then look at modern humanity in a quite different light. We shall not say that we possess absolute truth; we shall say that these men, our brothers, are now at a point where we also stood in the past. It is our duty to enter into what another person says; we need only make it clear to him that we value him at that stage of truth where he now stands. Everyone has to learn for himself, and thus we shall become tolerant towards every form of truth. We come to a better understanding of things; we do not battle against people but seek to live with them. Modern humanity has cultivated individual freedom. From out of this fundamental view of truth, Theosophy will develop an inner tolerance.

Love is higher than opinion. If people love one another, the most varied opinions can be reconciled. Hence it is deeply significant that in Theosophy no religion is attacked and no religion is specially singled out, but all are understood, and so there can be brotherhood because the adherents of the most varied religions understand one another.

This is one of the most important tasks for mankind today and in the future: that men should learn to live together and understand one another. If this human fellowship is not achieved, all talk of occult development is empty.

OCCULT DEVELOPMENT

You will have gathered from yesterday's study how important it is to develop a feeling of fellowship, which means overcoming all regard for your own Ego if you wish to penetrate more deeply into the spiritual life. For example, anyone who aspires to occult development must among other things get rid of the following form of egoism. He must not say: "What good is it for me to hear about occult things from others when I cannot see them for myself?" That implies a lack of trust. He must trust a person who has reached a certain stage of development. People work together, and if someone has achieved more than others, he will not have achieved it for himself alone but for all the others, and they are called upon to listen to him. By this means his own powers are enhanced, and his hearers, through the very fact of having first given him their trust, will gradually become able to gain knowledge for themselves. You should not want to take a second step before the first.

There are three paths of occult development: the Eastern, the Christian-Gnostic and the Christian-Rosicrucian, or simply the Rosicrucian. They are distinguished above all by the extent to which the pupil surrenders himself to his teacher. What, then, happens to a man who enters on occult development? What are the necessary preconditions for it?

Let us first consider the life of an ordinary man nowadays. From early till late he is occupied with his work and his daily experiences; he makes use of his intellect and his outer senses. He lives and works in what we call the waking state. But that is only *one* state; between waking and sleeping there is another. In this state he is aware of pictures, dream pictures, passing through his soul. These pictures are not directly related to the external world and ordinary reality. We may call this the dream-state, and it is interesting to study how it takes its course. Many people suppose that dreams are nonsense, but this is not so. Even with people today dreams have a meaning, but not that of experiences in waking life. When we are awake, our mental pictures always correspond to definite facts and experiences; in our dreams they do not. For instance, you may dream that you hear the clatter of horses' hooves, and when you wake up you realise that you were hearing the ticking of the clock by your bedside. Dreams are symbolic pictures. You may have a dream which tells a whole story. A student, for instance, may dream about a duel and all its preliminary details, from the request for pistols to the report of the shot which wakes him—and then he realises that he has knocked down the chair that stood by his bed. Or again, a peasant woman may dream that she is on her way to church; she enters; she hears the priest utter lofty sayings, with his arms moving; suddenly his arms turn into wings and then the priest starts to crow: she wakes up and hears the cock crowing outside!

You can see from these examples that in dreams we live in a very different sort of time from that of our waking consciousness. The actual cause of the dream I have quoted was the last event in point of time. The reason is that such a dream flashes through the soul in a moment and has its own inner time. You must picture it in this way: when you wake up and remember all the details, you extend this inner time yourself, so that the events seem to have occurred in that extended period. This will also help you to get some idea of how time appears in the astral world. A small experience thus creates a long dramatic course of events. The dream flashes through the soul in a moment and in a flash arouses a whole series of pictures. In this way you yourself transpose time into the dream.

Inner conditions may also be represented symbolically in dream: for instance, you may have a headache and dream that you are in a cellar with a lot of cobwebs. Or the beating of your heart or a feeling of being hot may be represented in a dream by a fiery stove. Some people who possess a particular inner sensitivity may have a different experience: they may dream, for instance, that they are in an unhappy situation. Here the dream is prophetic—a symbol of some latent illness which will come out in a few days' time. Many people even dream of the remedy for such an illness. In short, our manner of perception in dreams is quite different from that of ordinary life.

The third state is that of dreamless sleep, sleep without consciousness, when nothing comes before the soul. Now if you begin to be aware of higher worlds as a result of inner development, the first indication you will notice is that your dreams become more regular and meaningful. Above all, you will gain knowledge through your dreams, provided only that you pay careful attention to them. Later, you may notice that your dreams become more frequent, until you come to feel that you have been dreaming all night through. Again, you may notice that your dreams are concerned with things which do not exist at all in the outside world and which you cannot possibly experience physically. You will find that in your dreams you no longer see things which originate in the outer world or symbolic conditions such as those I described above, but, as I have just said, you will experience pictures of things which have no existence in the sense-world, and you will then notice that your dreams are saying something important. For instance, you may dream that a friend of yours is in danger from fire and you may see him getting nearer and nearer to the danger. The next day you may learn that this friend was taken ill during the night. You did not actually see him falling ill; you saw a symbolic picture of it. Thus your dreams may be influenced from higher worlds, so that you experience something which does not exist in the physical world; that is how impressions from higher worlds pass over into dreams. This is a very important bridge to higher occult development.

Someone might say that all this was only dreamt—how can any significance be read into it? But that is a wrong approach. Take the following example: it is said that Edison once dreamt how to make an electric light bulb; he remembered the dream and made the light bulb in accordance with it. Suppose someone had then come along and said: "The lamp is no good—it was only a dream". You can see that what matters is not the mere fact of dreaming but whether the dream has significance for life. Quite often dreams of this sort go unheeded because we fail to notice them. That is wrong; it is just these delicate points that we should attend to; then we shall make progress.

Later comes a stage when the nature of reality is disclosed to the pupil in dream, and he can then test the dream by the reality. When he has advanced so far that he has the whole picture-world present before him in daylight and not only during sleep, he is then able to analyse with his intellect whether what he sees is true. This means that it is wrong to use dream-pictures as a foundation for wisdom; the pupil must wait for them to enter into his daytime experience. If he exercises conscious control over them, a stage is soon reached when the pupil not only sees what is physically present but can truly perceive the astral element in a man, his soul and his aura. He then learns to understand what the shapes and colours in the astral body signify—what passions, for example, they express. So he learns gradually to spell out, as it were, the soul-world. But he must always realise that everything there is symbolical.

Here it might be objected that if you see symbols only, some particular event might be symbolised by all sorts of images, and you could never be sure that a given image has a consistent meaning. But when you reach a certain stage, one image always does stand for one thing, just as in the ordinary world one object is always represented by the same mental concept. For instance, you will find that a given passion is always represented for everyone by the same image. The important thing is to learn how to read the images correctly.

Now you can understand why the sacred books of all religions tend to speak almost entirely through symbolic images. Wisdom, for example, may be described as light: the reason is that to anyone who is occultly developed the wisdom of man and other beings always appears as astral light. Passions appear as fire. The ancient religious documents do not tell only of things on the physical plane, but also of events on higher planes; they owe their origin to seers and are concerned with higher worlds; hence they have to speak to us in pictures. Everything narrated from the Akashic Record has for the same reason been presented in pictures of this kind.

The next condition experienced by the pupils is called "continuity of consciousness". When an ordinary person is completely withdrawn from the sense-world in sleep, he is unconscious. This is no longer so with a pupil who has reached the stage just mentioned. By day and by night, with no interruption, he lives in a state of fully clear consciousness, even when his physical body is at rest.

After some time the pupil's entry into a new but quite specific state of consciousness is marked by the fact that sounds and words are added to the images. The images speak to him in an intelligible language. They tell him what they are, without any possibility of deception. These are the sounds and speech of Devachan, the Music of the Spheres. Everything speaks forth its own name and its relation to other things. This comes in addition to astral sight, and it marks the seer's entry into Devachan. Once a man has reached this Devachanic state, the lotus-flowers, the Chakrams or wheels begin to revolve at specific places in the astral body, turning like the hands of a clock from left to right. These are the sense-organs of the astral body, but their mode of perception is an active one. The eye, for example, is at rest; it allows the light to enter and only then perceives it. The lotus-flowers, on the other hand, perceive only when they are in motion and take hold of an object. The vibrations caused by the revolving lotus-flowers bring them into contact with the astral substance, and that is how perception on the astral plane occurs.

What are the forces which activate the lotus-flowers, and where do they come from? We know that during sleep the exhausted forces of the physical and etheric bodies are restored by the astral body; by its inherent regularity it can make up for irregularities in the physical and etheric bodies. It is these forces, normally used for overcoming fatigue, which animate the lotus-flowers. When a man enters on occult development, he is thus really withdrawing certain forces from his physical and etheric bodies. If these forces were to be withdrawn permanently from the physical body, the man would fall ill; he would find himself utterly exhausted. If therefore he does not want to injure himself, morally as well as physically, he must find something to replace these forces.

He must remind himself of the general rule: Rhythm restores power. Here you have an important occult principle. Most people today lead lives devoid of any regular rhythm, especially as regards their thoughts and their behaviour. Anyone who allowed the distractions of the outer world to gain a hold on him would be unable to avoid the dangers to which his physical body would be exposed in the course of his occult development by the withdrawal of these forces of renewal. Hence he has to strive to introduce a rhythmic element into his life. Of course he cannot arrange his days so that each day passes exactly like another. But he can at least pursue certain activities regularly, and indeed anyone who wants to develop on the occult path will have to do this. Thus he should, for example, do certain exercises of meditation and concentration at a chosen time every morning. He can also bring rhythm into his life if in the evening he reviews the events of the day in reverse order. If he can bring in further regularities, so much the better: in that way his life will take its course in harmony with the laws of the world. Everything in the system of nature is rhythmical—the course of the Sun, the passage of the seasons, of day and night, and so on. Plants, too, grow rhythmically. It is true that the higher we go in the kingdoms of nature, the less rhythm we find, but even in animals a certain rhythm can be observed: for instance, animals mate at regular times. Only man now leads an unrhythmical, chaotic life: nature has deserted him.

Man's task, therefore, is deliberately to infuse some rhythm into this chaotic life, and he has available certain means through which he can bring this harmony and rhythm into his physical and etheric bodies. Both these bodies will then gradually develop such rhythms that they will correct themselves when the astral body withdraws. If they are forced out of their proper rhythm during the day, they will of their own accord regain the right kind of movement when they are at rest.

The means available consist in the following exercises, which must be practised in addition to meditation:

I. *Thought control.* This means preventing, at least for a short time every day, all sorts of thoughts from drifting through the mind, and bringing a certain ordered tranquillity into the course of thinking. You must take a definite idea, set it in the centre of your thinking, and then logically arrange your further thoughts in such a way that they are all closely linked with the original idea. Even if you do this for only a minute, it can be of great importance for the rhythm of the physical and etheric bodies.

II. *Initiative in action.* You must compel yourself to some action, however trivial, which owes its origin to your own initiative, to some task you have laid on yourself. Most actions derive not from your own initiative but from your family circumstances, your education, your calling and so on. You must therefore give up a little time to performing actions which derive from yourself alone. They need not be important; quite insignificant actions fulfil the same purpose.

110

III. *Tranquillity.* Here the pupil learns to regulate his emotions so that he is not at one moment up in the skies and at the next down in the dumps. Anyone who refuses to do this for fear of losing his originality in action or his artistic sensibility can never go through occult development. Tranquillity means that you are master of yourself in the most intense pleasure and in the deepest grief. Indeed, we become truly receptive to the joys and sorrows of the world only when we do not give ourselves over egotistically to them. The greatest artists owe their greatest achievements precisely to this tranquillity, because through it they have opened their eyes to subtle and inwardly significant impressions.

IV. *Freedom from prejudice.* This, the fourth characteristic, sees good in everything and looks for the positive element in all things. Relevant to this is a Persian legend told of Christ Jesus. One day Christ Jesus saw a dead dog lying by the wayside; he stopped to look at the animal while those around him turned away in disgust. Then Jesus said: "What beautiful teeth the dog has!" In that hideous corpse he saw not what was ugly or evil but the beauty of the white teeth. If you can acquire this mood, you will look everywhere for the good and the positive, and you will find it everywhere. This has a powerful effect on the physical and etheric bodies.

V. *Faith.* Next comes faith, which in its occult sense implies something rather different from its ordinary meaning. During occult development you must never allow your judgment of the future to be influenced by the past. Under certain circumstances you must exclude all that you have experienced hitherto, so that you can meet every new experience with new faith. The occultist must do this quite consciously. For instance, if someone comes up to you and tells you that the church steeple is crooked and at an angle of 45 degrees, most people would say that is impossible. The occultist must always leave a way open to believe. He must go so far as to have faith in everything that happens in the world; otherwise he bars the way to new experiences.

You must always be open to new experiences; by this means your physical and etheric bodies will be brought into a condition which may be compared with the contented mood of a broody hen.

VI. *Inner Balance.* This is a natural outcome of the other five qualities. The pupil must keep the six qualities in mind, take his life in hand, and be prepared to progress slowly in the sense of the proverb about drops of water wearing away a stone.

Now if anyone acquires higher powers through some artificial means without attending to all this, he will be in a bad way. In ordinary life today the spiritual and the physical are intermingled, somewhat like a blue and yellow liquid in a glass of water. Occult development sets going a process rather like the work of a chemist who separates the two liquids. Soul and body are separated in a similar way, and the benefits of the mingling are lost. An ordinary person, because the soul stays in close relation to the body, is not subjected to the more grotesque passions. But as a result of the separation I have been talking about, the physical body, with all its attributes, may be left to itself, and this can lead to all manner of excesses. Thus a man who has embarked on occult development, but has not taken care to cultivate moral qualities, may manifest certain traits which as an ordinary man he had long ago ceased to exhibit. He may suddenly become a liar, vengeful, quick to anger; all sorts of characteristics which had previously been toned down may appear in a violent form. This may happen even if someone who has neglected moral development becomes unduly absorbed in the teachings of Theosophy.

We have seen that a man must first pass through the stage of spiritual sight and only then comes to the stage of spiritual hearing. While he is still at the first stage he has of course to learn how the images are related to their objects. He would find himself plunged into the stormy sea of astral experiences if he were left to fend for himself. For this

112

reason he needs a guide who can tell him from the start how these things are related and how to find his bearings in the astral world. Hence the need to find a Guru on whom he can strictly rely. In this connection three different ways of development can be distinguished.

1. *The Eastern way,* also called *Yoga.* Here, an initiated man living on the physical plane acts as the Guru of another, who entrusts himself to his Guru completely and in all details. This method will go best if during his occult development the pupil eliminates his own self entirely and hands it over to his Guru, who must even advise him on every action he may take. This absolute surrender of one's own self suits the Indian character; but there is no place for it in European culture.

2. *The Christian way.* Here, in place of individual Gurus, there is one great Guru, Christ Jesus Himself, for everyone. The feeling of belonging to Christ Jesus, of being one with Him, can take the place of surrender to an individual Guru. But the pupil has first to be led to Christ by an earthly Guru, so that in a certain sense he still depends on a Guru on the physical plane.

3. *The Rosicrucian way,* which leaves the pupil with the greatest possible independence. The Guru here is not a leader but an adviser; he gives directions for the necessary inner training. At the same time he takes good care that, parallel with the occult training, there is a definite development of thinking, without which no occult training can be carried through. This is because there is something about thinking which does not apply to anything else. When we are on the physical plane, we perceive with the physical sense only what is to be found on that plane. Astral perceptions are valid for the astral plane; devachanic hearing is valid only in Devachan. Thus each plane has its own specific form of perception. But one activity—logical thinking—goes through all worlds. Logic is the same on all three planes. Thus on the physical plane you can learn something which

113

is valid also for the higher planes; and this is the method followed by Rosicrucian training when on the physical plane it gives primary attention to thinking, and for this purpose uses the means available on the physical plane. A penetrative thinking can be cultivated by studying theosophical truths, or by practising mental exercises. Anyone who wishes further training for the intellect can study books such as *Truth and Science,* and *The Philosophy of Freedom,* which are written deliberately in such a way that a thinking trained by them can move with certainty on the highest planes. Even a person who studies these books and knows nothing of Theosophy might find his way about in the higher worlds. But, as I have said, the teachings of Theosophy act in the same way.

Here, then, the Guru is only the friend and adviser of the pupil, for by training his reason the pupil will be training the best Guru for himself. But he will of course still need a Guru to advise him on how to make progress in freedom.

Among Europeans, the Christian way is best suited to those whose feelings are most strongly developed. Those who have more or less broken away from the Church and rely rather on science, but have been led by science into a doubting frame of mind, will do best with the Rosicrucian way.

ORIENTAL AND CHRISTIAN TRAINING

Yesterday we concluded by outlining the three methods of occult development: the Eastern, the Christian and the Rosicrucian. Today we will begin by going more closely into the details which distinguish these three paths. But first I should say that no occult school sees in its teaching and requirements anything like a moral law valid for all mankind. The requirements apply only to those who deliberately choose to devote themselves to a particular occult training. You can, for instance, be a very good Christian and fulfil everything that the Christian religion prescribes for the laity without undergoing a Christian occult training. It goes without saying that you can be a good man and come to a form of the higher life without any occult training.

As I said earlier, the Eastern training calls for strict submission to the Guru. I will describe briefly the kind of instruction that an Eastern teacher gives. You will realise that the actual instructions cannot be given publicly; I can indicate only the stages of the path. The instructions can be divided into eight parts:

1. Yama	5. Pratyahara
2. Niyama	6. Dharana
3. Asanam	7. Dhyanam
4. Pranayama	8. Samadhi

1. *Yama* includes all the abstentions required of anyone who wishes to undergo Yoga training: Do not lie, do not kill, do not steal, do not lead a dissolute life, desire nothing.

The injunction, *Do not kill,* is very stringent and applies to all creatures. No living creature may be killed or even injured, and the more strictly this rule is observed, the further will the pupil progress. Whether this rule can be observed in our civilisation is another matter. Every killing, even of a flea, impedes occult development. Whether someone is obliged to do it—that again is a different question.

You will understand the command, *Do not lie,* if you recall what I said about the astral plane, where to lie is to kill and every lie is a murder. Lying therefore comes into the same category as killing.

The precept, *Do not steal,* also has to be applied most strictly. A European might claim that he does not steal. But the Eastern Yogi does not look at it so simply. In the regions where these exercises were first promulgated by the great teachers of humanity, conditions were much simpler: stealing was easy to define. But a Yoga teacher would not agree that Europeans do not steal. For example, if I unjustifiably appropriate another man's labour, or if I procure for myself a profit which may be legally permissible but which involves the exploitation of another person—all this the Yoga teacher would call stealing. With us, social relations have become so complex that many people violate this commandment without the slightest awareness of doing so. Suppose you have money and deposit it in a Bank. You do nothing with it; you exploit no-one. But suppose now the banker starts speculating and exploits other people with your money. In the occult sense you will be responsible for it, and the events will burden your karma. You can see that this precept requires deep consideration if you are entering on a path of occult development.

With regard to the injunction, *Do not lead a dissolute life,* take a person with private means whose capital is invested without his knowledge in a distillery; he is just as culpable as the producer of strong drinks. The fact that he knew nothing about it makes no difference to his karma. There is only one way of keeping to the right path with these abstentions: strive to need nothing. Even if you have great possessions, in so far as you strive to have no needs, you will injure no-one.

The injunction, *Desire nothing,* is especially hard to carry out. It means that the pupil must strive to have no needs, no desire for anything in the world, and to do only what the outer world demands of him. He must even suppress any feeling of pleasure at doing good to someone; he must be moved to help not by any such feeling but simply by the sight of suffering. And if he has to spend money, he must not think of his own wishes or desires but must say to himself: "I need this to maintain my body or to meet the needs of my spirit, as everyone else does. I do not desire it, but am considering only how best to live my life in the world."

In Yoga training this concept of *Yama* is, as I have said, taken most strictly; it could not be transplanted to Europe as it stands.

2. *Niyama.* This means the observance of religious customs. In India, where these rules are chiefly applied, a problem is solved which causes many difficulties in European civilisation. For us it is very easy to say that we have passed beyond dogmas; we hold to the inner truth only and have no use for outer forms. The further a European has got away from religious observances, the more exalted does he imagine himself to be. The Hindu takes the opposite view; he holds firmly to the rites of his religion, and no-one may touch them, but anyone is free to form his own opinion of them. There are sacred rites, which have come down from very ancient times and signify something very profound. An uneducated man will have very elementary ideas about them; a more highly cultured man will have different and better ideas, but no-one will say that anyone else's ideas are wrong. The wise and the unlearned observe the same customs. There are no dogmas, only rites. Hence these deeply religious customs can be observed by all, and in them the wise and the simple are brought together. Thus the rites are socially unifying. No-one is restricted in his opinions by conforming to a strict ritual.

The Christian religion has followed the opposite principle. Not customs, but opinions, have been imposed on people, and the consequence is that formlessness has become the rule in our social life. So begins a complete disregard of all observances that could draw human beings together; every form that expresses symbolically a higher truth is gradually rejected. This is a great loss for human development, especially for development in the Eastern sense.

In Europe today there are plenty of people who think they have learnt to do without dogmas, yet it is precisely the free-thinkers and the materialists who are the worst fanatics for dogmas. The dogma of materialism is much more oppressive than any other. The infallibility of the Pope is no longer valid for many people, but instead we have the infallibility of the Professor. Even the most liberal-minded, whatever they may say to the contrary, are victims of the dogmas of materialism. Think of the dogmas which burden lawyers, doctors and so on. Every university Professor teaches his own dogma. Or think how people suffer from the dogma of the infallibility of public opinion, of the newspapers! The Eastern teacher of Yoga does not demand that the ceremonies which unite the learned and unlearned together should be abandoned: these sacred ancient rites are symbols of the highest wisdom. No culture is possible without such formal observances; to believe otherwise is an illusion. Suppose for instance a colony is founded with no forms or accepted customs. Clearly a colony such as that, with no church, no religious services or observances, could exist quite well for a time, because its people would continue to live in accordance with the rules and conventions they had brought with them. But as soon as these were lost, the colony would collapse, for every culture must embody a certain pattern which will give expression to its inner character. Modern civilisation must recover the forms it has lost; it must learn again how to give external expression to its inner life. In the long run social life is conditioned by its pattern, its formal customs. The ancient sages knew this, and hence they held firmly to religious practices.

3. *Asanam* means the adoption of a certain bodily pos-

118

ture in meditation. This is much more important for the Oriental than for the European, because the European body is no longer so sensitive to the flow of certain subtle currents. The body of the Oriental is even nowadays more delicately organised; it responds readily to the currents which pass from East to West, from North to South, from the Heights to the Depths. Spiritual currents flow through the universe, and it is for this reason that churches are built with a particular orientation. It is for this reason also that the Yoga teacher makes his pupil adopt a special posture; the pupil has to keep his hands and feet in a particular position, so that the currents may flow through his body in the right direction. If the Hindu did not bring his body into this harmony, he would risk losing all the benefits of his meditation.

4. *Pranayama* is breathing, yoga-breathing. It is an essential and detailed part of Eastern Yoga training. Christian training pays almost no attention to it, but in Rosicrucian training it has regained some importance.

What does breathing signify in occult development? You can find the answer in the injunctions not to kill and not to injure any living creature. The occult teacher says: "By breathing you are slowly, continually, killing your surroundings." What does this mean? We breathe the air in, use it to furnish our blood with oxygen and then breathe it out again. What does this involve? We inhale the air with its oxygen; we combine the oxygen with carbon and we exhale carbon dioxide, in which no man or animal can live. We breathe in oxygen and breathe out carbon dioxide, which is a poison; and this means that with every breath we draw we are dealing death to other beings in our environment. Bit by bit we are killing our whole environment: we inhale the breath of life and exhale air which we can make no further use of. The occult teacher is concerned to alter this. If there were only men and animals in the world, all the oxygen would soon be used up and all living creatures would die. It is thanks to the plants that this does not happen, for in plants the breathing process is the reverse of ours. They

119

assimilate carbon dioxide, separate the carbon from the oxygen, and use the carbon to build up their bodies. They liberate oxygen, and men and animals breathe it in again. So do the plants renew the life-giving air; otherwise all life would long ago have been destroyed. We owe our life to the plants, and in this way plants, animals and men are complementary.

But this process will change in the future, and since anyone who is undergoing occult training must begin to do what others will achieve at some time in the future, he must learn not to kill with his breath. That is *Pranayama,* the science of the breath. Our modern materialistic age places health under the sign of fresh air; but our modern way of achieving health through fresh air is one that terminates in death. A Yogi, on the other hand, will retire into a cave and as far as possible will breathe the air he has himself exhaled—unlike the European, who is always wanting to open windows. A Yogi has learnt the art of contaminating the air as little as possible because he has learnt how to use it up. How does he do it? The secret has always been known to the European occult schools, where it was called the finding of the Stone of the Wise, the Philosopher's Stone.

At the turn of the eighteenth to the nineteenth century a good deal of information about occult development leaked out. The Stone of the Wise was often mentioned in published writings, but one can see that the author understood little of it, even though it all came from the right sources. In 1797 a local Thuringian newspaper printed an article about the Stone of the Wise which included, *inter alia,* the following: "The Stone of the Wise is something one has only to recognise, for every man has seen it. It is something which everyone holds in his hand for part of almost every day, but without knowing that it is the Philosopher's Stone." This is an enigmatic way of indicating that the Philosopher's Stone can be found everywhere. Yet this strange expression is literally true.

This is how it comes about: The plant, as it builds up its

body, takes in the carbon dioxide and retains the carbon for its body-building purposes. Men and animals eat the plants, take in the carbon, and give it up as carbon dioxide when they breathe out. So we have a carbon cycle. In the future there will be a great change. Man will learn to extend the range of his innate powers and will gradually come to do for himself what at present he leaves to the plant. Just as man passed through the plant and animal kingdoms in the course of his evolution, so will he in a certain sense retrace his steps. He will himself become plant; he will take up the plant-nature into himself and accomplish the whole plant-process within himself. He will retain the carbon dioxide and will consciously build up his body with it, as the plant now builds up its own body unconsciously. He will prepare the necessary oxygen in his own organs, unite it with carbon to form carbon dioxide, and then deposit the carbon again in himself. Thus he will be able to build up his bodily structure. Here is an idea which opens up a great perspective for the future; and when it comes about man will cease to be a killer with his breath.

Now we know that carbon and diamond are the same substance; diamond is more thoroughly crystallised and a more transparent form of carbon. Hence we need not think that in the future people will go about looking like negroes. Their bodies will consist of soft, transparent carbon. At that stage man will have found the Philosopher's Stone and he will transform his own body into it.

Anyone undergoing occult development has to anticipate this process as far as possible. He must deprive his breath of the capacity to kill, and must organise his breathing so that the air he exhales is usable and can be breathed again. How is this to be accomplished? You have to bring rhythm into your breathing. The teacher gives the necessary instructions. Breathing in, holding your breath and breathing out again—this must be done rhythmically, if only for a short period. With every rhythmical exhalation the air is improved slowly but surely. Here the old saying applies—drops of

121

water wear away the stone. The chemists cannot yet confirm this: their instruments are too coarse to detect the finer substances, but the occultist knows that breath imbued with rhythm is life-promoting and contains more than the normal amount of oxygen. The breath can be purified also, and at the same time, by meditation. This, too, contributes, if only by a very little, towards bringing the plant-nature back into man, so that he may become a being who does not kill.

5. *Pratyahara,* the curbing of sense-perception. Nowadays in ordinary life a person receives a continual stream of sense-impressions and allows them all to work on him. The occult teacher says to the pupil: "You must concentrate on a single sense-impression for a specified number of minutes and pass on to another only by your own free choice."

6. *Dharana,* when the pupil has done that for a while he must learn to make himself deaf and blind to all sense-impressions; he must turn away from them and try to hold in his thought only the concepts they leave behind. If he thus lives in concepts only, and controls his thoughts and links one concept to another by his own free choice, he has reached the condition known as *Dharana.*

7. *Dhyanam.* There are concepts—often disregarded by Europeans—which do not derive from sense-impressions. We have to form them for ourselves—mathematical concepts, for example. No perfect triangle exists in the outer world; it can only be conceived in thought, and the same is true of a circle. Then there is a whole range of concepts which anyone undertaking occult training must study intensively. They are symbolic concepts which are connected with some objects—for example, the hexagram, or the pentagram, symbols which occultism can explain. The pupil must keep his mind sharply concentrated on such symbolic objects, not to be found in the outer world. It is the same with another kind of concept: for example, that of the species Lion, which can be laid hold of only in thought. On these, too, the pupil must focus his attention. Finally, there are moral

ideas, such for example as the following, from *Light on the Path:* "Before the eye can see, it must be incapable of tears." This, too, cannot be experienced outwardly, but only inwardly. This meditation on concepts which have no sense-perceptible counterpart is called *Dhyanam.*

8. Finally, *Samadhi,* the most difficult of all. After concentrating for a very long time on an idea which has no sense-perceptible counterpart, you allow your mind to rest in it and your soul to be filled with it. Then you let the idea go, so that nothing is left in your consciousness. But you must not fall asleep, as would then normally happen; you must remain conscious. In that state the secrets of the higher worlds begin to reveal themselves. This state can be described as follows. You are thinking, for you are conscious, but you have no thoughts, and into this thinking without thoughts the spiritual powers are able to pour their content. But as long as you yourself fill your thinking, they cannot come in. The longer you can hold in your consciousness this activity of thinking without thoughts, the more will the supersensible world reveal itself to you.

These are the eight realms with which a teacher of Eastern Yoga deals.

Now we will speak about the Christian way of occult training, as far as this is possible, and we shall see how it differs from the Eastern way. This Christian way can be followed with the advice of a teacher who knows what has to be done and can rectify mistakes at every step. But in Christian training the great Guru is Christ Jesus Himself. Hence it is essential to have a firm belief in the presence and the life on Earth of the Christ. Without this, a feeling of union with Him is impossible. Further, we must recognise that in the Gospel of St. John we have a document which originates with the great Guru Himself and can itself be a source of instruction. This Gospel is something we can experience in our own inner being and not something we merely believe. Whoever has absorbed it in the right way will

123

no longer need to prove the reality of Christ Jesus, for he will have found Him.

In Christian training you must meditate on this Gospel, not simply read and re-read it. The Gospel begins: "In the beginning was the Word, and the Word was with God and the Word was God . . . " The opening verses of this Gospel, rightly understood, are sentences for meditation and must be inwardly absorbed in the condition of *Dhyanam,* as described above. If in the morning, before other impressions have entered the soul, you live for five minutes solely in these sentences, with everything else excluded from your thoughts, and if you continue to do this over the years with absolute patience and perseverance, you will find that these words are not only something to be understood; you will realise that they have an occult power, and you will indeed experience through them a transformation of the soul. In a certain sense you become a clairvoyant through these words, so that everything in St. John's Gospel can be seen with astral vision.

Then, under the direction of the teacher, and after meditating again on the five opening verses, the pupil allows the first chapter to pass through his mind for seven days. During the following week, after again meditating on the five opening verses, he goes on to the second chapter, and so in the same way up to the twelfth. He will soon learn how powerful an experience this is; how he is led into the events in Palestine when Christ Jesus lived there, as they are inscribed in the Akashic Record, and how he can actually experience it all. And then, when he reaches the thirteenth chapter, he has to experience the separate stages of Christian Initiation.

The first stage is the Washing of the Feet. We must understand the significance of this great scene. Christ Jesus bends down before those who are lower than himself. This humility towards those who are lower than we are, and at whose expense we have been able to rise, must be present everywhere in the world. If a plant were able to think, it would thank the minerals for giving it the ground on which it can

124

lead a higher form of life, and the animal would have to bow down before the plant and say: "To thee I owe the possibility of my own existence." In the same way man should recognise what he owes to all the rest of nature. So also, in our society, a man holding a higher position should bow before those who stand lower and say: "But for the diligence of those who labour on my behalf, I could not stand where I do." And so on through all stages of human existence up to Christ Jesus Himself, who bows down in meekness before the Apostles and says: "You are my ground, and to you I fulfil the saying, 'He who would be first must be last, and he who would be Lord must be the servant of all'." The Washing of the Feet betokens this willingness to serve, this bowing down in perfect humility. This is a feeling that everyone committed to occult development must have.

If the pupil has permeated himself with this humility, he will have experienced the first stage of Christian Initiation. He will know by two signs, an outer and an inner, that he has gone thus far. The outer sign is that he feels as though his feet were being laved with water. The inner sign is an astral vision which will quite certainly come: he sees himself washing the feet of a number of persons. This picture rises up in his dreams as an astral vision, and every pupil has the same vision. When he has experienced it, he will have truly absorbed this whole chapter.

The second stage is that of the Scourging. When the pupil has reached this point, he must, while he reads of the Scourging and allows it to act upon him, develop another feeling. He must learn to stand firm under the heavy strokes of life, saying to himself: "I will stand up to whatever pains and sorrows come to me." The outer sign of this is that the pupil feels a kind of prickling pain all over his body. The outer sign is that in a dream-vision he sees himself being scourged.

The third stage is that of the Crowning with Thorns, and for this he has to acquire yet another feeling: he learns to stand firm even when he is scorned and ridiculed because of all that he holds most sacred. The outer sign of this is that he experiences a severe headache; the inward symptom is that he has an astral vision of himself being crowned with thorns.

The fourth stage is that of the Crucifixion. A new and quite definite feeling must be developed. The pupil must cease to regard his body as the most important thing for him; his body must become as indifferent to him as a piece of wood. He then comes to look quite objectively on the body he carries with him through life; it has become for him the wood of the Cross. He need not despise it, any more than he does any other tool. The outer sign for having reached this stage is that during the pupil's meditation red marks (stigmata) appear at those places on his body which are called the sacred wounds. They do indeed appear on the hands and feet, and on the right side of the body at the level of the heart. The inward sign is that the pupil has a vision of himself hanging on the Cross.

The fifth stage is that of the Mystical Death. Now the pupil experiences the nothingness of earthly things, and indeed dies for a while to all earthly things.

Only the most scanty descriptions can be given of these later stages of Christian Initiation. The pupil experiences in an astral vision that darkness reigns everywhere and that the earthly world has fallen away. A black veil spreads over that which is to come, and while he is in this condition the pupil comes to know all that exists as evil and wickedness in the world. This is the Descent into Hell. Then he experiences the tearing away of the curtain and the world of Devachan appears before him. This is the rending of the veil of the Temple.

The sixth stage is that of the Burial. Just as at the fourth stage the pupil learnt to regard his own body objectively, so now he has to develop the feeling that everything else around him in the world is as much part of what truly belongs to him as his own body is. The body then extends far beyond its skin; the pupil is no longer a separate being;

he is united with the whole planet. The Earth has become his body; he is buried in the Earth.

The seventh stage, that of the Resurrection, cannot be described in words. Hence occultism teaches that the seventh stage can be conceived only by a man whose soul has been entirely freed from the brain, and only to such a man could it be described. Hence we cannot do more than mention it here. The Christian teacher indicates the way to this experience.

When a man has lived through this seventh stage, Christianity has become an inner experience of the soul. He is now wholly united with Christ Jesus; Christ Jesus is in him.

ROSICRUCIAN TRAINING–THE INTERIOR OF THE EARTH–EARTHQUAKES AND VOLCANOES

Yesterday we described the various stages by which pupils of the Eastern and the Christian occult schools came to higher knowledge. Today I will try to describe, in a similar way, the stages of Rosicrucian training.

You must not imagine that the Rosicrucian training contradicts the other two. It has existed since the fourteenth century, and it had to be introduced because mankind then needed a different form of training. Among the Initiates it was foreseen that a time would come when because of the gradual increase of knowledge men would be confused in matters of religious faith. Therefore a form of instruction had to be created for those who felt within themselves the discord between faith and knowledge. In the Middle Ages the most learned men were also those of the greatest faith and piety; and for a long time afterwards those who had made headway in scientific knowledge could not conceive of any contradictions between knowledge and faith. We are usually told that faith was shaken by the ideas of Copernicus, but that is quite wrong: after all, Copernicus dedicated his book to the Pope! It is only in quite recent times that this conflict has gradually developed. The Masters of Wisdom saw that this was bound to happen and that a new path would have to be found for those whose faith had been destroyed. For persons much occupied with science, the necessary path towards Initiation is the Rosicrucian, for the Rosicrucian method shows that the highest knowledge of mundane things is thoroughly compatible with the highest knowledge of spiritual truths. It is precisely through the Rosicrucian path that those who have been led away from Christian belief by what they take to be science can learn to understand Christianity truly for the first time: By this method anyone can come to a deeper grasp of the truth of Christianity. Truth is one, but it can be reached along different paths, just as at the foot of a mountain there are various paths, but they all meet at the summit.

The essence of Rosicrucian training may be described in two words: true self-knowledge. The Rosicrucian pupil has to distinguish two things, not merely theoretically but practically, so that they become part of his everyday life. There are two forms of self-knowledge—the lower form, called by the Rosicrucian pupil "self-mirroring", which should serve to overcome the lower self, and the higher form of self-knowledge which is born out of self-renunciation.

What is the lower form of self-knowledge? It consists in the recognition of our everyday self, of what we are and of what we bear within us: in other words, an examination of our own soul-life. But we must make it quite clear to ourselves that by this means we cannot reach the higher self. When we look into ourselves we see only what we are, and that is just what we have to grow out of in order to surmount the ordinary self. But how is this to be done? Most people are convinced that their characteristics are the best, and anyone who lacks these characteristics is uncongenial to them. Once a person has outgrown this idea, not only in theory but in feeling, he will be on the way to true self-knowledge.

You can get out of the habit of self-admiration by a particular method which can be practised whenever you have five minutes for it. You must start from the principle that all characteristics are one-sided; you must learn to recognise in what respects yours are one-sided and then try to balance them. This principle may not amount to much in theory, but in practice it is highly effective. If you are industrious, you must ask yourself whether your activity may not be wrongly applied. Quickness, too, is one-sided; it needs to be supplemented by careful deliberation. Every quality has

129

its polaric opposite; you should cultivate its opposite and then try to harmonise the two extremes. For example, make haste slowly; be quick and yet deliberate; deliberate and yet not slow. Then the pupil will begin to grow beyond himself. All this is not part of meditation, but must be acquired alongside it.

It is by attention to small details that this harmony can be achieved. If your tendency is not to let anyone finish what he is saying, you must keep a watch on yourself and make up your mind that for six weeks you will keep silent, as far as possible, when someone else is talking. Then you must accustom yourself to speak neither too loudly nor too softly. Things such as this, which are generally not thought of, contribute essentially to inner self-development, and the more attention you pay to quite insignificant characteristics, the better it will be. If you try not only to acquire certain moral, intellectual or emotional qualities, but to get rid of some external habit, this will be particularly effective. It is a question not so much of investigating your inner self as of endeavouring to perfect the qualities which you have not yet fully developed, and to complement those you already have by cultivating their polaric counterparts. Self-knowledge is one of the hardest things to acquire, and it is precisely those who think they know themselves best who are most likely to be deceived: they think too much about themselves. You should get out of the habit of fixing your attention on yourself and constantly using the word "I"— "I think, I believe, I consider this right". Above all you must get rid of the notion that your opinion is worth more than that of other people. Suppose, for instance, that someone is very clever. If he displays his cleverness in the company of people who are not so clever, his behaviour will be very ill-timed; he will be doing it only to please his own egoism. He ought to adapt his response to the needs and capacities of others. Agitators are particularly apt to offend against this rule.

In addition to all this you must cultivate patience, in the

occult sense of the word. Most people who want to achieve something cannot wait; they imagine they are already fit to receive anything. This patience derives from strict self-training, and it, too, is related to the lower form of self-knowledge.

Higher self-knowledge begins only when we can say that our higher self is not in our ordinary "I". It is in the whole great world outside, in the sun and the moon, in a stone or an animal: everywhere can be found the same essential being that is in us. If a man says: "I wish to cultivate my higher self and to withdraw from the world; I want to know nothing about anything material", he entirely fails to understand that the higher self is everywhere outside, and that his own higher self is only a small part of the Great Self outside. Certain methods of so-called "spiritual" healers make this mistake, which can be very serious. They instil into patients the idea that matter has no real existence and so there can be no illnesses. This notion is based on a false self-knowledge, and, as I have said, it can be very dangerous. This healing method calls itself Christian, but in fact it is anti-Christian.

Christianity is an outlook which sees in everything a revelation of the Divine. Everything material becomes an illusion unless we look on it as an expression of the Divine. If we disown the external world, we are disowning the Divine; if we reject the material realm, in which God has revealed himself, we are rejecting the Divine. The important thing is not to gaze into ourselves, but to seek to know the Great Self which shines down into us. The lower self says: "Standing here I am cold." The higher Self says: "I am also the cold, for as part of the one Self I live in the cold and make myself cold." Again the lower self says: "I am here in the eye which beholds the sun." The higher Self says: "I am in the sun and in the sun's rays I look into your eyes."

Really to go out of yourself is to renounce yourself. Hence the Rosicrucian training aims at drawing the lower self out of man. In the early days of Theosophy the gravest mistake was made when people were told to look away from the external world and to gaze into themselves. That is a great illusion, for then we find only the lower self, the fourth principle, which imagines itself to be divine but is not so at all. We must come out of ourselves if we are to know the Divine. "Know thyself" means also "Overcome thyself".

The Rosicrucian training leads its pupils through the following stages, and these go hand in hand with the six exercises already mentioned: control of thought; initiative in action; tranquillity; lack of prejudice, or positiveness; faith; and inner balance. The training itself consists of the following:

1. *Study*. Without study, a modern European cannot get to know himself. He must try, first of all, to reproduce in himself the thoughts of the whole of humanity. He must learn to think in harmony with the world-order. He must say to himself: "If others have thought this, it must be a possible human thought; I will test whether one can live with it." He need not swear to it as a dogma, but by studying it he must get to know what it is. The pupil must learn about the evolution of sun and planets, of the earth and humanity. Thoughts of this kind, given to us for study, purify the spirit. By following the strict lines of these thoughts, we come to form strictly logical thoughts ourselves. This kind of study, again, purifies our thoughts, and so we learn to think with strict logic. If, for instance, we are reading a difficult book, the most important thing is not to comprehend its whole content, but to enter into the author's line of thought and learn to think with him. Hence the pupil should find no book too difficult; if he does, it means only that he is too easy-going to think.

The best books are those we have to take up again and again, books we cannot understand immediately but have to study sentence by sentence. It does not matter so much what we study as how we study. If we study the great truths, for instance the planetary laws, we develop an important line of thought, and this is what really matters. If we say that we want more moral teaching and nothing about planetary systems, we show great egoism. True wisdom engenders a moral life.

2. *Imagination or Imaginative Knowledge* is the second thing we have to attain. What is it and how do we achieve it? As we go through the world we must observe it in the light of Goethe's saying: "Everything transitory is but a symbol." Goethe was a Rosicrucian and he can lead us into the life of the soul. Everything must become for us a symbol in manifold respects. Suppose, for instance, we are walking past an autumn crocus: in form and colour it is a symbol of mourning. Another flower, the convolvulus, is a symbol of helplessness; another flower, with its splash of red, is a sign of gaiety, and so on. A bird with bright colours may be a symbol of coquetry. The symbols may actually be expressed in the names: weeping willow, forget-me-not, and so on. The more we reflect in this way, so that external things become symbolic pictures of moral qualities, the more easily shall we attain to Imaginative Knowledge. We can see similar likenesses in human beings. For instance, we can study people's temperament from their gait—look at the slow, heavy step of the melancholic, the light, springy step of the sanguine type.

After some time spent on these exercises we can pass to exercises of real Imagination. Take, for example, a living plant, look at it carefully, sink yourself into it, then draw forth the inner feeling of your soul and lay it as it were in the plant, as is described in the book, *Knowledge of the Higher Worlds*. All this stimulates the Imagination, and by this means the pupil acquires astral vision. After a time he will notice a little flame proceeding from the plant: that is the astral counterpart of its growth. Again, the pupil takes a seed and visualises the whole plant, as it will later on be in reality. These are exercises of the Imagination; by their means one comes to see things surrounded by their astral element.

3. The third stage is called *learning the occult script.* There is in fact such a script, through which one can penetrate more deeply into things. An example will show you more exactly what I mean. With the close of the old Indian civilisation a new civilisation began. The symbol for such an evolutionary stage is the vortex. These vortices exist everywhere in the world. They occur in the nebulae—the Orion nebula, for instance. There, too, an old world is dying and a new one being born. When the Indian civilisation was coming into being, the Sun was in the sign of Cancer; during the Persian civilisation in Gemini; during the Egyptian civilisation in Taurus; during the Graeco-Roman civilisation in Aries. Since the astronomical sign for Cancer is ♋ = ♋ , this was the sign for the rise of the Indian civilisation.

Another example is the letter M. Every letter of the alphabet can be traced back to an occult origin. Thus M is the symbol of wisdom; it derives from the shape of the upper lip ⌣⌣ . It is also the sign for the waves of the seas 〰 ; hence wisdom may be symbolised by water. These signs indicate sounds which correspond with real things, and in the Rosicrucian training such studies are cultivated.

4. A *rhythmical element* is brought into breathing. It plays a less important part than it does in Eastern training, but it belongs to the Rosicrucian training and a Rosicrucian knows that through meditation the air he breathes out is purified.

5. The *correspondence between Microcosm and Macrocosm* is emphasised. This means the connection between the great world and the small, or between man and the world outside him.

Man has emerged by gradual stages and his various members have been formed in the course of evolution. Now it is impossible for certain organs to arise in a being which has, for example, no astral body, and therefore they could not come into existence on the Sun, even in a preliminary form.

The liver is an instance of this: it cannot exist without the etheric body, but it is actually created by the astral body. Similarly, no being can have warm blood unless it first appeared at a time when the Ego was at least in course of preparation. True, the higher animals are warm-blooded, but they split off from man when the development of his Ego was already on the way. Hence we can say that the liver is closely related to the astral body, and warm blood to the Ego. In fact every one of man's organs, even the smallest, has its specific relationship to one member of his being. If the pupil concentrates his attention on himself objectively, as though on something outside himself—if for instance he concentrates on the point at the root of the nose and connects with it a particular saying given by his occult teacher, he will be guided to that which corresponds to this point and he will come to know it. If he concentrates on this point under definite guidance, he will come to know the nature of the Ego. Another, much later exercise is directed towards the inner part of the eye; through this one learns to know the inner nature of light and of the sun. The nature of the astral can be learnt by concentrating on the liver, with the aid of certain specific words.

This is true self-development, when the pupil is taken out of himself by means of each organ on which he concentrates his attention. This method has become specially important in recent times because humanity has become deeply involved in matter. In this way one penetrates through the material to its creative cause.

6. Dwelling in, or sinking oneself into, the Macrocosm. This is the same form of spiritual contemplation that we described as *Dhyanam*. The pupil sinks himself into the organ he is contemplating—for example, the inner part of the eye. After concentrating on it for a while, he drops the mental picture of the external organ and thinks only of that to which the eye leads him—the light. In this way he comes to the creator of the organ and so out into the Macrocosm. He then feels his body increasingly growing larger and larger

until it is as large as the Earth; indeed even bigger than the Earth, until all things are in it. And then he lives in all things.

7. The seventh stage corresponds to the Eastern *Samadhi*. It is called divine blessedness, because now the pupil ceases to think of this last concept, but he retains the power to think. The content of his thought falls away, but the activity of thought remains. And thus he comes to rest in the divine-spiritual world.

These stages of Rosicrucian training are more inward, and call for a subtle cultivation of the higher life of the soul. The widespread superficiality of our material epoch is a powerful obstacle to the necessary deepening of the whole inner life; it must be overcome. This form of training is particularly well suited to Europeans. Anyone who is in earnest can carry it out. But Goethe's saying, "It is indeed easy, but even the easy is hard", applies here.

We have gone into the various methods of training, and I will end these lectures by showing you something of the relationship between man and the whole Earth, so that you will see how man is related to everything that happens on Earth.

I have described the evolution of man and shown you how he can acquire a true inner being of his own. In the course of evolution the whole of humanity will attain to everything that the individual can achieve through occult training. But what will be happening to the Earth while mankind is developing in this way? There is a great difference between the Earth seen by the occultist and the Earth known to the ordinary geologist or scientist. He looks on it as merely a sort of great lifeless ball, with an interior not very unlike its exterior, except that at most the interior substances are fluid. But it is not easy to understand how such a lifeless ball could have produced all the different kinds of beings on it.

We know that on this Earth of ours various phenomena

occur which deeply affect the fate of many people; but present-day science looks on this as a purely external relationship. Thus the fate of hundreds and thousands may be affected by an earthquake or a volcano. Does the human will have any influence on this, or is it all a matter of chance? Are there dead laws which act with blind fury, or is there some connection between these events and the will of man? What is really happening when a man is killed by an earthquake? What does the occultist say about the interior of the Earth?

The occult science of all epochs says the following about the interior of the Earth. We must think of the Earth as consisting of a series of layers, not completely separated from one another like the skins of an onion, but merging into one another gradually.

1. The topmost layer, the mineral mass, is related to the interior as an eggshell is to the egg. This topmost layer is called the Mineral Earth.

2. Under it is a second layer, called the Fluid Earth; it consists of a substance to which there is nothing comparable on Earth. It is not really like any of the fluids we know, for these all have a mineral quality. This layer has specific characteristics: its substance begins to display certain spiritual qualities, which consist in the fact that as soon as it is brought into contact with something living, it strives to expel and destroy this life. The occultist is able to investigate this layer by pure concentration.

3. The "Air-Earth". This is a substance which annuls feelings: for instance, if it is brought into contact with any pain, the pain is converted into pleasure, and vice versa. The original form of a feeling is, so to speak, extinguished rather as the second layer extinguishes life.

4. The "Water-Earth", or the "Form-Earth". It produces in the material realm the effects that occur spiritually in Devachan. There, we have the negative pictures of physical things. In the "Form-Earth" a cube of salt, for example,

would be destroyed, but its negative would arise. The form is as it were changed into its opposite; all its qualities pass out into its surroundings. The actual space occupied by the object is left empty.

5. The "Fruit-Earth". This substance is full of exuberant energy. Every little part of it grows out at once like sponge; it gets larger and larger and is held in place only by the upper layers. It is the underlying life which serves the forms of the layers above it.

6. The "Fire-Earth". Its substance is essentially feeling and will. It is sensitive to pain and would cry out if it were trodden on. It consists, as it were, entirely of passions.

7. The "Earth-mirror" or "Earth-reflector". This layer gets its name from the fact that its substance, if one concentrates on it, changes all the characteristics of the Earth into their opposites. If the seer disregards everything lying above it and gazes down directly into this layer, and if then, for example, he places something green before him, the green appears as red; every colour appears as its complementary opposite. A polaric reflection arises, a reversal of the original. Sorrow would be changed by this substance into joy.

8. The "Divisive" layer. If with developed power one concentrates on it, something very remarkable appears. For example, a plant held in the midst of this layer appears to be multiplied, and so with everything else. But the essential thing is that this layer disrupts the moral qualities also. Through the power it radiates to the Earth's surface, it is responsible for the fact that strife and disharmony exist there. In order to overcome this disruptive force, men must work together in harmony.

That is precisely why this layer was laid down in the Earth—so that men should be enabled to develop harmony for themselves. The substance of everything evil is prepared and organised there. Quarrelsome people are so constituted that this layer has a particular influence on them. This has been known to everyone who has written out of a true knowledge of occultism. Dante in his *Divine Comedy* calls this layer the Cain-layer. It was here that the strife between the brothers Cain and Abel had its source. The substance of this layer is responsible for evil having come into the world.

9. The "Earth-core". This is the substance through whose influence black magic arises in the world. The power of spiritual evil comes from this source.

You will see that man is related to all the layers, for they are continually radiating out their forces. Humanity lives under the influence of these layers and has to overcome their powers. When human beings have learnt to radiate life on Earth and have trained their breathing so that it promotes life, they will overcome the "Fire-Earth". When spiritually they overcome pain through serenity, they overcome the "Air-Earth". When concord reigns, the "Divisive" layer is conquered. When white magic triumphs, no evil remains on Earth. Human evolution thus implies a transformation of the Earth's interior. In the beginning the nature of the Earth's body was such as to hold subsequent developments in check. In the end, when human powers have transformed the Earth, it will be a spiritualised Earth. In this way man imparts his own being to the Earth.

Now there are occasions when the very substance of the passions of the Fire-Earth begins to rebel. Aroused by men's passions, it penetrates through the Fruit-Earth, forces its way through the channels in the upper layers and even flows up into and violently shakes the solid Earth: the result is an earthquake. If this passion from the Fire-Earth thrusts up some of the Earth's substance, a volcano erupts. All this is closely connected with man. In Lemurian times, the upper layer was still very soft and the Fire-layer was near the surface. Human passions and the "passion-substance" of this layer are related; when men give rein to evil passions they strengthen its passions, and that is what happened at the end of Lemurian times. Through their passions the Lemurians made the Fire-Earth rebellious, and in this way they brought the whole Lemurian continent to destruction. No other cause for this destruction could be found except in what they had themselves drawn forth from the Earth. Today the layers are thicker and firmer, but there is still this connection between human passion and the passion-layer in the interior of the Earth; and it is still an accumulation of evil passions and forces that gives rise to earthquakes and volcanic eruptions.

How man's destiny and will are related to happenings in the Earth can be seen from two examples which have been occultly investigated. It has been found that persons who have been killed in an earthquake appear in their next incarnation as men of high spiritual quality and faith. They had progressed far enough to be convinced by that final stroke of the transitoriness of earthly things. The effect of this in Devachan was that they learnt a lesson for their next lives: that matter is perishable but spirit prevails. They did not all come to realise that, but many of them are now living as people who belong to some spiritual-theosophical movement.

In the other example, the births which occurred during a time of frequent earthquakes were investigated. It was found that all those born at about the time of an earthquake, though not exactly in its area, were, surprisingly enough, men of a very materialistic cast of mind. The earthquakes were not the cause of this; rather it was these strongly materialistic souls, ripe for birth, who worked their way down into the physical world by means of their astral will and let loose the forces of the Fire-Earth layer, which proceeded to shake the Earth at the time of their birth.

Man transforms his dwelling-place and himself at the same time, and when he spiritualises himself, he spiritualises the Earth also. One day, at a later planetary stage, he will have ennobled the Earth by his own creative power. Every moment when we think and feel, we are working on the great structure of the Earth. The Leaders of mankind have insight into such relationships and seek to impart to men the forces which will work in the true direction of evolution. One of the latest of these impulses is the Theosophical Movement. Its purpose is to develop harmony and balance in the very depths of the human soul. Anyone who puts the assertion of his own opinion higher than love and peace has not thoroughly understood the idea of Theosophy. The spirit of love must penetrate even into the opinions a man holds. In the course of occult development he must unavoidably learn this, or he will get no further. He must renounce entirely his own opinions and must wish to be solely an instrument of the objective truth which comes from the spiritual world and flows through the world as the one great Truth. The more a man renounces himself and sets his own opinions aside, becoming instead a channel for the great Truth, the more does he manifest the true spirit of Theosophy.

All this is extraordinarily difficult today. But theosophical teaching is itself a promoter of peace. When we come together so that we may live within this teaching, it gives rise to peace. But if we introduce something from outside, we bring dissension in, and that should really be an impossibility. So the theosophical conception of the world must pass over into feeling—into something I would call a spiritual atmosphere—in which Theosophy lives. You must have a will to understand; then Theosophy will hover like a unifying spirit over our gatherings, and from there will spread its influence out through the world.

NOTES FROM ANSWERS TO QUESTIONS

Stuttgart,
2nd September, 1906

Question about the work of the Ego

Work can be done on the astral body, on the etheric body, on the physical body. Every human being works on his astral body; all moral education is work on the astral body. Even when a person enters on the process of Initiation, on occult training, he has still much work to do on his astral body. Initiation leads to stronger work on the etheric body through the cultivation of aesthetic pleasure and of religion. The Initiate works consciously on his etheric body.

Astral consciousness is four-dimensional in certain connections. In order to form an approximate idea of this, the following may be said. Anything that is dead has the tendency to remain in its three dimensions. Anything living extends all the time beyond the third dimension. Anything that grows has, through its movements, the fourth dimension within its three dimensions. If something moves in a circle, and if the circle it traces goes on increasing in size, we come at last to a straight line. But the straight line will not return to its starting point, because our world is three-dimensional. In astral space, a line does return, because astral space is closed on all sides. It is quite impossible, there, to go straight on for ever. Physical space is open to the fourth dimension. Height and breadth are two dimensions; the third dimension leads out into the fourth. In astral space a different geometry prevails.

Why are theosophists still so inadequate?

One should not allow a personal element to enter into one's judgments. An objective assessment of things should be the aim.

About conditions in Devachan

Pain and grief are external in Devachan. You do not experience your own pains there. Pain is something you look at. You see it as thunder, as lightning, as colour. That is blessedness. You are looking at pictures of happenings caused by others here below. A peaceful condition in Devachan depends on the lives of people between birth and death. Harmony here on Earth brings about peace in Devachan. A man lives continuously in the three worlds. "Rest in peace!" is not quite right.

Is there any value in reading Masses for the dead?

Good thoughts are balm for the dead. It is not selfish love that we should send them, not mourning because we no longer have them here; this harms a dead person and weighs on him like lead. But love that endures, which does not lay claim to the dead person by wanting him back again—this nourishes him and augments his happiness.

Remorse?

Remorse has no value. But one must make good for harm done; this shortens the Kamaloka period.

On communion with loved ones in Kamaloka

It is clearer, more definite, in Devachan, for in Kamaloka consciousness is clouded by the paying off of debts incurred through personal guilt.

Lotus-flowers?

The lotus-flowers are inner movements, within the human being.

If one is out of harmony with one's parents, what is the reason for it?

To be out of harmony with one's parents is generally something determined by karma.

What does the astral body look like?

When the astral body is together with the physical body, it is somewhat egg-like in shape. After death it is a wonderfully radiant, mobile formation. In accordance with individual characteristics it has various colours, radiant colours. Its three gleaming points are at first widely separated, joined together but open below. They are centres of force; they draw progressively together and then they look like a small triangle.

1. Heart; 2. Liver; 3. Brain. These three points work together at the time of a new incarnation. In Devachan they are radiant centres of force, which streams out from the three points. In the astral world these three points form a triangle; in Devachan they form a six-pointed figure—two interlaced triangles. They are bells.

A question was asked about the *"permanent atom"* often spoken of in theosophical circles at that time.

Atoms are a speculation. Hence we avoid speaking about them, for they are only an assumption. One should not think about things which are not facts; human beings should only look and observe.

Can one look into the future?

This is possible, but the occultist refrains from doing so, because, almost always, it behoves only a high Initiate to know the future. The Initiate's prevision does not determine what another person does; the latter will act in the future entirely out of his free will.

On family connections

Families with a strong family tradition are subject to a quite definite law, whereby the family karma is worked out. The ancestor upholds the family until he can build a new body for his own next incarnation. The continuity and cohesion of the family depends on the blood.

On Art

Art is the revelation of hidden laws of nature. Goethe says: "The beautiful is a manifestation of hidden laws of nature which would otherwise remain forever concealed." Nature can realise her intentions only up to a certain stage; man can bring them to expression, but the artist has to leave out the blood and life.

On Group-Souls

At a later, much later, time the Group-Souls will embark on the same experiences that humanity undergoes today. They will eventually build individual bodies for themselves. They will become single individuals, each with an individual soul. Animals will never give rise to men, but human beings— of a kind quite different, certainly, from ourselves—will develop out of the Group-Souls. The human stages—the Saturn stage, the Sun stage, the Moon stage, the Earth stage, and so on—can be gone through in the most varied ways.

What is your attitude to the Lord's Prayer?

The primal Christian prayer is: Lord, let this cup pass from me; nevertheless not my will, but thine, be done. One should not pray egotistically. Prayer should be a raising up of oneself into the spiritual world, a source of strength and invigoration.

On marriage

Marriage is a duality. In the world today there is a prevailing tendency to lead everything back, quite wrongly, to the sexual. A great antithesis plays into the realm of marriage: the husband has a female etheric body and the wife a male etheric body. The spirit and soul in the man is more feminine, and vice-versa. The human soul strives towards the highest. Hence the man will equate the highest with the womanly, because his soul is feminine. The external part, the body, is only an outer symbol, only a parable. "All things transient are but a parable." "The eternal-womanly draws us to the heights."

On the Ego-body

The Ego-body appears to the clairvoyant as a blue hollow between the eyes, behind the forehead. When a person begins to work on it, rays stream out from this point.

On the nature of comets

A comet is an assemblage of Kama, desire-substance, without the corresponding spiritual substance. The comet gets as far only as the astral body. The visibility of comets arises from the powerful friction caused by the astral body passing through etheric substance.

How does gold arise?

We have first the four ethers:

Fire	Fire ether
Air	Light ether
Water	Chemical ether
Earth	Life ether

No life can arise without Life ether, which fills out the bodies. Each ether can be cooled so that it becomes solid. In earlier times gold flowed in clefts; earlier still it was gaseous; it was Fire ether, Light ether. The rays which come to us from the Sun were formerly etheric substance. All the gold was once Sun ether, Light ether. Gold is densified Sun ether, densified sunlight; silver is densified moonlight.

Which beings inhabit the Moon?

The Moon is inhabited by those physical beings who have

remained behind at an earlier stage of evolution: Luciferic beings. On the Old Moon there were beings who had fallen so far into evil that they could not take part in further evolution. They established themselves on the Moon. These malevolent beings are evident especially in the waning Moon; when the Moon is waxing they are less harmful. Some dreadful beings inhabit the Moon, but there are also favourable beings, actively concerned with growth and birth.

On the Book of Revelation

The Book with Seven Seals in the Revelation of John is written by man himself. His evolution and involution are inscribed there. The first writing in it applies to the seven sub-races. Each sub-race writes and seals a page of it. When the next sub-race emerges, the page is unsealed.

On the difference between cremation and burial

The difference exists chiefly for the etheric body. Cremation provides correctly for the dissolution of the physical body into cosmic space. "Decaying" *(verwesen)* means a return to one's being. *(Wesen)*.

On the life of Jesus

The life of Jesus is at the same time a fact and a symbol. Proof of his life can be given only by Spiritual Science. You will not find any historical proofs, for the Christ was not known as a high Initiate to the writers of those days.

On the inner Word

The inner Word reveals itself after a man has already attained astral sight. Then he enters into the Devachan condition; then he hears the world-secrets sounding in himself; and then he hears the name that belongs to each thing. Later, his own name will be spoken to the Initiate, and to meditate on it is especially effective. That, then, is the inner Word. The Initiate is thereby awakened, and this inner Word is a sure guide for his later development.

NOTES FROM ANSWERS TO QUESTIONS

Stuttgart,
4th September, 1906

In earlier times man's etheric body was still outside his physical body, and so also, of course, was his Ego-consciousness. His soul worked on the physical body from outside. The horse today has its etheric body still outside.

How did the names of the zodiacal constellations originate?

The whole animal kingdom was once within man; this means that he was at a stage between the human realm and the animal kingdom of today. In order to be able to develop further, he had to separate off from himself those parts which could not go with him. He separated the parts which form the animal kingdom of today. Originally, therefore, the animals were much less sharply differentiated from man than they now are. They have gradually degenerated.

The separating off of the animal kingdom did not occur suddenly, but by slow degrees. First the fishes were separated, then the reptiles and amphibians, then the birds and the mammals. And within each group the separating off was again gradual: thus the beasts of prey, for example were separated earlier than the apes.

When the lions were separated, the constellation in which the Sun then stood was called Lion, and when the bull-nature was separated, the relevant constellation was called Bull. The names of the four apocalyptic creatures in the Revelation of John—Eagle, Lion, Bull, Man—point in the same direction. But the names of all the zodiacal constellations are not thereby explained.

The Moon in earlier times—before the Earth separated

from it—consisted of soft plant-substance, like living peat or spinach-pulp, penetrated by a woody structure which has today hardened into rock. In this soft substance lived the Moon-plants, real plant-animals, halfway between the plants and the animals of the present-time. Then the Earth separated, bringing into being the four kingdoms of nature—minerals, plants, animals and men—some of the plant-animals failed to transform themselves completely into present-day plants. The sponges arose in this way.

"Before the voice can speak in the presence of the Masters, it must have lost the power to wound." (From *Light on the Path,* by Mabel Collins.)

When we send forth a loving thought, it creates a wonderfully beautiful thought-form, like a flower which gently opens and then surrounds the person to whom the thought applies. Anyone who thinks a thought full of hate creates a sharp-pointed angular form, closed at its apex, designed to wound. That which is here called "the Masters" is the divine voice which speaks in us. It speaks constantly, but we do not always allow it to emerge. The thought-form of love is open; hence the voice of the Masters can sound through it. But the closed thought-form of hate leaves the divine thought-form no way out, so that it has to remain unheard.

In the astral, a lie is a murder

Suppose I think the following thought: I met a man. A quite definite thought-form will be engendered by that. Now to someone else I say it again: I met a man. The same thought-form is again engendered. The two thought-forms meet and strengthen each other. But if I tell a lie and say: I did not meet a man—this engenders a thought-form opposed to the first. The result is an explosion in the astral body of the liar.

How can one protect one's astral body against bad influences?

The best way is to be sure and true oneself. As a special

149

protection you can create through forcible concentration of the will an astral sheath, a blue, egg-shaped mist. You must say to yourself firmly and emphatically: "Let all my good qualities surround me like a coat of mail!"

Why did the first Christians have the Fish as their symbol, besides the Lamb?

Among the fishes, especially Amphioxus, the spinal marrow began to take form. Man was once at the stage when he had the fish nature still within himself; he was wholly a soul-being and worked on his body from outside. Then he separated the fishes from himself. Later on the brain was formed out of the spinal marrow.* In this way man becomes a Self. But the Self is ennobled by Christianity and hence the Fish is the symbol for the early Christians. The story of Jonah indicates the same thing. Jonah—man—is at first outside the fishes: this means the soul working on the body from the outside. Then he becomes a Self and enters into the fish—the physical body. Through Initiation the physical body is again left aside.

Can physical objects be seen after death?

After death we see nothing physical, but the corresponding astral images, astral and devachanic counterparts. The mineral realm is absent; it appears as an empty space, like a photographic negative. In Devachan one can see a clock, for a human design enters into it. All human artifacts can be seen there.

	Atma	transformed physical body
	Buddhi	transformed etheric body
	Manas	
Kama Manas	Ego	
Kama	Astral body	
Prana	Etheric body	
	Physical body	

*Goethe already knew this. Dr. Steiner found the relevant pencil sketch drawn in a notebook while he was working in the Goethe Archives in Weimar.

150

The universal flow of life is called Prana. It flows like water; but if it is given form by being poured into the physical body, rather as water is poured into a jug, then one speaks of the etheric body. The general astral substance, desire-stuff, is called Kama. If it is given the form of a body, one speaks of the astral body. The Ego is the centre of the person. Kama plays into it, and Manas also. Thus the Ego comprises a mixture of Kama and Manas. The Kama has to be completely transformed and ennobled, so that Manas may develop from it. If the etheric body is ennobled, Buddhi emerges; and Atma arises from the ennoblement of the physical body.

		The Mental Plane
	VII	Causal body
Arupa	VI	Causal body
	V	Causal body
		Akasha Chronicle
	IV	Etheric sphere
	III	Airy sphere
Rupa	II	Oceanic sphere, like the blood in a human body
	I	Continental realm

The continental realm embraces everything physical; the oceanic realm, everything living; the airy sphere, the whole range of feelings; and the etheric sphere, all thoughts. At the boundary of the etheric sphere is the Akasha Chronicle. It contains everything that has ever been thought. On the far side of the Akasha Chronicle lies everything that has not yet become thought. All new thoughts, all discoveries and so on, come from the Arupa region. Anyone who has developed Kama Manas comes after death as far as the etheric sphere, to thoughts that exist independently. The Ego shapes the astral body, so that Manas develops out of it. All Manas which has not yet been drawn into the astral is Arupa.

Denial and affirmation of life

Schopenhauer says that the world has been built by irrational will. Therefore the reason has to destroy the irrational will, so that the world goes to ruin. Schelling, Hegel and Fichte represent a different standpoint which can be expressed in the words: "From God—to God!" Let us consider the denial and affirmation of life through a parable. I show someone a piece of magnetised iron, and I tell him that in the iron resides an invisible force, called magnetism. He replies: I want to know nothing about this force; I affirm the iron. It is much the same if someone, looking only at the things of the world, says that he affirms the world. Certainly he affirms the world, but he denies the invisible forces within it. Life is truly affirmed only by someone who seeks for spiritual realities. Anyone else denies half of life. Many theosophists say: I don't bother about the world; I am concerned only to develop my higher self. In fact they are seeking only the lower man. The higher man is everywhere outside. If I feel the whole world in myself, then I have found my higher Self. My Self is outside me. Knowledge of the world is self-knowledge!

How does suggestion work?

Suggestion works on the Ego. The higher bodies are drawn out of the physical body, and then the Ego-body, without the physical brain, unconsciously follows the hypnotiser. The physical brain, the controller of actions, is detached. With an Initiate it is different. He retains conscious control without the aid of the physical brain, and so he cannot be hypnotised.

The "Pistis Sophia"

This book, written in the Coptic language, contains much of the discourses of Christ at the initiation of His disciples, and many inner expositions of parables. The thirteenth chapter is especially important. The ἁιμαρμένη (Haimarmene) is Devachan. The entire supersensible world is divided into twelve aeons. These are the seven divisions of the astral plane and the five lowest divisions of Devachan. Aberrated spirits can be purified from out of Devachan. The light-bearing purifier before Christ was Melchisedek. He is meant when we read of light coming from the ἐπίσγοπος (episko-pos). By ἄρχοντες (Archontes), the powers of evil are to be understood.

Conflict and arguing are not a realm for Theosophy. We should not squander time uselessly on disputes, but should speak only to those who have the heart and mind for Theosophy.

Why does Christ say: "I am the Way, the Truth and the Life", when previous great founders of religion had already pointed to the Way?

We must first transpose ourselves into past ways of speaking. In former times the spiritual content of speech was perceived at the same time as the words were heard. Then we can reflect on the following: Christ was the embodiment of the Second Person of the Godhead. No previous founder of a religion had embodied in himself the fullness of the Logos. But the divine element that His predecessors had embodied was a part of the Logos, and so of Christ Himself. Therefore Christ embraces everything previous to Him in the words, "I am the Way, the Truth and the Life".

Then one can take these words literally, in yet another sense. The previous founders of religions had shown the Way and taught the Truth, but they did not live out the Mystery of the Godhead in the sight of men. Hence they could say, "I am the Way and the Truth". Christ alone could say: "I am the Way, the Truth and the Life."

Now Elias means "Way", and Moses, "Truth". At the Transfiguration, Elias and Moses appeared with Christ. Hence the Transfiguration says: I am the Way, the Truth and the Life. The passing of Buddha into Nirvana, his death, is the same as the Transfiguration of Christ. At the moment when Buddha brought his working to an end, the real work-ing of Christ, His *Life*, begins.

153

REFERENCES

Note on the text. An authentic transcript of this lecture-course (Cycle I) is not available. For this printing we have followed essentially the transcript made by a member of the audience.

Page

7   *Jean-Jacques Rousseau,* 1712-1778, philosopher, critic of society.

7   *Jacob Boehme,* 1575-1624, mystic.

8   *Johannes Trithem,* Abbot of Sponheim, near Kreuznach, 1462-1516.

12 *Jean Paul Friedrich Richter,* 1763-1825, poet.

13 *Chela* (Tschela) Sanskrit. The pupil of a teacher of occult knowledge.

15 *Helen Keller,* 1880-1968, American writer. At the age of nineteen months she became blind and deaf.

15 *"a teacher of genius":* Miss Anne Mansfield Sullivan (Mrs. Macy).

15 *"Optimism",* an essay by Helen Keller, 1903.

16 *Subba Row* (Rao), 1856-1890, a learned Indian. He wrote articles for the journal, *The Theosophist,* which were later collected and published under the title, *Esoteric Writings,* second edition, 1931, Adyar, Madras.

18 *Arthur Schopenhauer,* 1788-1860, philosopher. The quoted sentence is the motto affixed to his "Prize Essay on the Foundation of Morality", 30 January, 1840. His essay, "On the Will in Nature", 1836, contains the sentence: "The upshot is easy, but to provide a foundation for morality is difficult."

20 *Tat tvam asi.* Sanskrit, from the Vedas.

20 *Pythagoras,* Greek philosopher, sixth century B.C.

20 *Johann Wolfgang Goethe,* 1749-1832.

23 *Julius Caesar,* 100 - 44 B.C.

31. *Theophrastus Paracelsus von Hohenheim,* 1493-1541.

32 *Francis of Assisi,* 1181-1226.

32 *Helena Petrovna Blavatsky,* 1831-1891, known in theosophical circles as H.P.B. See the section, "Reincarnation" in *Isis Unveiled,* Chapter X.

38 *"Goethe says . . . "* Literally, "And so the eye is formed by the light for the light.

38 *Johannes Kepler,* 1571-1630, astronomer and mathematician. Established the three laws concerning the movements of the planets.

38 *Galileo Galilei,* 1564-1642. Laid the foundations of mechanics, discovered the laws of free fall, of the pendulum, of ballistics.

40 *Michelangelo Buonarroti,* 1475-1564. His "Moses", intended for the tomb of Pope Julius II, is in the church of S. Pietro in Vincoli, Rome.

47 *Lipikas, Maharajas.* High spiritual Beings concerned with birth and destiny.

50 *Aristotle,* 384-322 B.C. The sentence cited here is from the treatise, "On the Poetic Art", Chapter 4.

53 "A book will be published": "The Education of the Child from the Standpoint of Spiritual Science", given as a lecture in various places in Germany; first published, made into an article, in Rudolf Steiner's periodical, *Lucifer-Gnosis,* 1907, and in the same year as a pamphlet. An English translation is available, entitled, *The Education of the Child in the Light of Anthroposophy.*

65 *Bach.* Among the children of Johann Sebastian Bach, 1685-1750, were three sons, as well-known musicians: Friedemann Bach, 1710-1784; Philip Emanuel Bach, 1714-1788; Johann Christian Bach, 1735-1782.

65 *Bernoulli,* a family of mathematicians, Basle. Jacob Bernoulli, 1654-1705; Nicholas Bernoulli, 1687-1759; Daniel Bernoulli, 1700-1782.

67 *Charles Darwin,* 1809-1882.

69 *Antoine Fabre d'Olivet,* 1768-1825, author of *"La Langue hébraique restituée",* 1816.

70 *Lorenz Oken,* 1779-1851, natural scientist and philosopher.

73 *Immanual Kant,* 1724-1804.

80 *Arupa:* Sanskrit, "without form", indicating the highest realm of Devachan.
    Rupa: Sanskrit, "form". The Rupa planes are the lower spheres of Devachan.

80 *"In the 'Secret Doctrine' ".* H. P. Blavatsky's "The Secret Doctrine".

81 *Plato,* 427-347 B.C.
    ". . . as Plato puts it." In the dialogue, *Timaeus.*

91 *Manasaputras.* Described in Blavatsky's "Secret Doctrine" as "Sons of Wisdom, who at the creation endowed mankind with Manas."

101 *Nicholas Copernicus,* 1473-1543, originator of the modern astronomical world-picture.

101 *Ptolemy,* 87-165, geographer and astronomer. For him the Earth was stationary at the centre of the universe.

107 *Thomas Alva Edison,* 1847-1931.

108 *"Everything that has been recounted from the Akasha Chronicle".* The reference is to the communications "From the Akasha Chronicle" published by Rudolf Steiner in his journal, *Lucifer-Gnosis,* from July 1904 to May 1908. Collected edition, Dornach, 1964. English translation published in America with the title: *Cosmic Memory: Prehistory of Earth and Man.*

110 *"at one moment up in the skies and at the next down in the dumps".* From Klärchen's song in Goethe's *Egmont,* 3,2.

111 *"a Persian legend."* See Goethe: Notes and comments for a better understanding of the *West-Östlicher Divan,* "Allgemeines".

112 *Guru.* In oriental Initiation, he who guides the pupil's occult development; leader on the path of knowledge.

115 *"The form of instruction in oriental schooling."* From the old Indian classic, "The Yoga-Sutras of Patanjali".

122 *"Light on the Path",* written down by Mabel Collins.

132 *". . . with the six qualities already mentioned."* See Lecture Twelve.

133 *"All things transient are but a parable".* Goethe's *Faust,* Part II, Act V, Chorus Mysticus.

133 *Knowledge of the Higher Worlds. How is it achieved?* Appeared as articles in *Lucifer-Gnosis,* June 1904 to September 1905; first published in book form, 1909. Collected Edition, Dornach, 1961. Sixth English edition, 1969. Revised by C.D. and D.S.O.

136 *"Certainly it is easy, but the easy is difficult."* Spoken by Mephistopheles in *Faust,* Part II, Act I, The Emperor's Palace.

138 *Dante Alighieri,* 1265-1321. The Divine Comedy, Inferno, Canto 32.

A short list of relevant publications of the works of Rudolf Steiner, not necessarily all in print at any one time.

Knowledge of the Higher Worlds. How is it achieved?
A Road to Self Knowledge. The Threshold of the Spiritual World
Manifestations of Karma
Occult Science — An Outline
Theosophy. An introduction to the supersensible knowledge of the world and the destination of man
The Theosophy of the Rosicrucian
Between Death and Rebirth
Links Between the Living and the Dead
Man as Symphony of the Creative Word
Supersensible Man

Full catalogue available from Rudolf Steiner Press
35, Park Road, London NW1 6XT

COMPLETE EDITION

of the works of Rudolf Steiner in the original German. Published by the *Rudolf Steiner Verlag, 4143 Dornach, Switzerland.*

General Plan (abbreviated):

A. WRITINGS

I. Works written between the years 1883 and 1925.

II. Essays and articles, written between 1882 and 1925.

III. Letters, drafts, manuscripts, fragments, verses, meditative sayings, inscriptions, etc.

B. LECTURES

I. Public Lectures

II. Lectures to Members of the Anthroposophical Society on general anthroposophical subjects.

Lectures to Members on the history of the Anthroposophical Movement and the Anthroposophical Society.

III. Lectures and Courses on special branches of work.

Art: Eurythmy, Speech and Drama, Music, Visual Arts, History of Art.

Education

Medicine

Science

Sociology and the Threefold Social Order.

Lectures given to Workmen at the Goetheanum.

The number of lectures amounts to some six thousand, shorthand reports of which are available in the case of the great majority.

C. REPRODUCTIONS AND SKETCHES

Paintings, drawings, coloured diagrams, eurythmy forms, etc.

A Complete Bibliographical Survey (with subjects, dates and places where the lectures were given) is available. This, together with all the volumes of the edition, can be obtained from the Rudolf Steiner Bookshops in London, and directly from the *Rudolf Steiner Verlag* (address as above) by the trade.